All You Need...
for Advanced VCE

Business

Business
Finance

Author: Neil Reaich
Series Editor: Jenny Wales

Letts Educational
The Chiswick Centre
414 Chiswick High Road
London W4 5TF
Tel: 020 8996 3333
Fax: 020 8842 7956
www.letts-education.com

First published 2001

Text © Neil Reaich 2001

Editorial, design and production by Hart McLeod, Cambridge
Illustrations by Roger Langridge and Lisa Smith

A CIP record for this book is available from the British Library

ISBN 184085619 X

Printed and bound in the UK

Letts Educational Limited, a division of Granada Learning Limited.
Part of the Granada Media Group.

Contents

What's the point of records?

You need to understand why it is important for a business to create and maintain accurate financial records and to know about different users of financial information.

'What do you mean we're in a mess? Come on Jack, business is booming and we just can't sell enough. I've just taken on two more employees.'

'Brenda, you have no financial control over the business. Your paperwork is lousy. Money is being wasted left, right and centre and that money is your profit. In fact you are hardly making any money.'

'I've been really too busy running the business to worry about the paperwork.'

'Yes, you've not even looked at your recent bank statements. Soon you won't have money to pay the bills. That's why the bank want to interview you.'

Work it out

1 Why does Brenda believe her business is doing well?

2 Why does her financial adviser, Jack, disagree?

3 What does the financial adviser mean by money being wasted?

4 What might be the consequences of not making improvements to her financial system?

KEEPING RECORDS

Paperwork in a business is really all about keeping accurate records of:

■ its expenditure – or everything it buys;

■ its income – or everything it sells.

Many businesses now keep their records in computer spreadsheet files. This allows the business to check the accuracy of their records easily. The data entered in one cell will automatically update another and spreadsheets are linked to each other. What's more, the data can be put into graphs to provide an easier way of looking at how well the business is performing. Finally, you can search the data to bring up exactly the information you desire, e.g. overdue payments. Brenda had no real knowledge of her business. She couldn't tell Jack any of the following information.

■ How much was ordered from her suppliers in the last month.

■ Who her suppliers were.

■ How much was still owed to them and how much of this was beyond the agreed payment time.

■ What she was owed by her customers and how much of this was overdue.

■ What money she may need to run her business over the next few months.

■ How well her business was performing for the money and effort she had put into it.

There may also have been some errors in the orders, deliveries and money received or paid out. It is important to check on these.

WHAT'S GONE WRONG?

Hatrick staff know that all is not well.

'I ordered 1 batch of 5 rolls of textiles not 5 batches.'

'Our customer has only paid us £200.50 instead of £2005.00.'

'They ordered 5 items, but we delivered 10.'

'They have delivered 20 items and only charged for 2.'

'Who gave permission to buy that many?'

'Well, this lot of textiles we bought are the wrong colour.'

Work it out

1 How may each error have come about?
2 Which errors are the fault of the business?
3 Which errors will cost the business money if they are not put right?
4 Even when errors are corrected there are costs. Why?

Errors need to be corrected even if they are in your favour. Why do you think this is necessary?

WHAT'S THE POINT AGAIN?

Accurate records:

- are essential to help a business check on errors and to monitor how well it is doing by providing evidence for the accounts;

- will provide information that will help managers make decisions about the future;

- can support businesses wanting to raise money;

- improve investors' confidence;

- add to the trust between buyer and seller;

- are legally needed for the Companies Acts and Partnership Agreements and help provide accurate information for assessment of taxes.

Ordering and delivering

What's it all about?

You need to understand the key financial documents needed for orders and deliveries and why they are used.

Cash book

Money received				Money paid			
Date	Details	Amount	Type of payment	Date	Details	Amount	Type of payment
28/5	Casual customers	£90.45	Cash	28/5	Rent to Council	£289.00	Cheque
29/5	Shops	£216.87	Cheque	28/5	Postage	£35.78	Cash
29/5	Casual customers	£68.98	Cash	29/5	Materials	£198.00	Cheque

Work it out

Brenda is having a bad day. Can you help her?

1 What is the total sum paid out during the two days?

2 What is the sum received?

3 What is the balance for the two days?

4 If Brenda were worried about having enough cash to pay the bills what could she have done?

Brenda has been told to keep accurate records and know how to check on them. She must sort out the paperwork into date order and check these against entries into the cash book. This records all the money coming into and going out of the business.

WHAT ARE THE DOCUMENTS?

It is not as simple as just keeping a **cash book**. There are many key documents that a business needs to receive, send out and record. The documents are linked together. Receiving one document will lead to another being set up or altered. The documents include those shown below.

Some documents are sent out from customers to suppliers and some are sent from suppliers to customers. Copies of each are kept by the businesses. Employees in different departments may have a responsibility in processing the forms and may need to make records available to other departments.

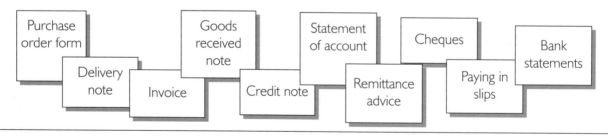

Purchase order form • Delivery note • Invoice • Goods received note • Credit note • Statement of account • Remittance advice • Cheques • Paying in slips • Bank statements

GETTING THE ORDERS SORTED AND DELIVERED

Let us take a closer look at how the documents may be triggered when placing an order.

'Hatrick', a hat and cap making business, wants to buy more textile materials. It has already asked for quotations from suppliers and chooses S&B Textiles as the preferred supplier. The purchasing department sends out a **purchase order form** to the supplier, A&B Textiles.

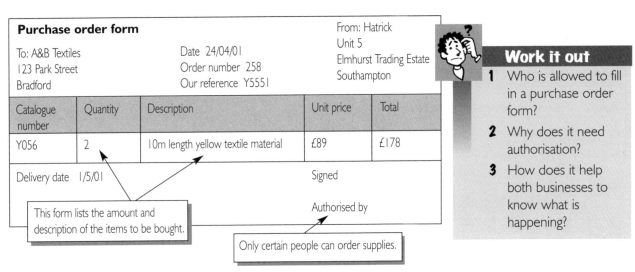

Work it out

1 Who is allowed to fill in a purchase order form?

2 Why does it need authorisation?

3 How does it help both businesses to know what is happening?

Purchase order form

To: A&B Textiles
123 Park Street
Bradford

Date 24/04/01
Order number 258
Our reference Y5551

From: Hatrick
Unit 5
Elmhurst Trading Estate
Southampton

Catalogue number	Quantity	Description	Unit price	Total
Y056	2	10m length yellow textile material	£89	£178

Delivery date 1/5/01

Signed

This form lists the amount and description of the items to be bought.

Authorised by

Only certain people can order supplies.

The supplier sends a **delivery note** with the goods to the warehouse where Leslie in the 'goods in department' at Hatrick checks the order against the goods. The person delivering the order will ask Leslie to sign the delivery note when he has checked the delivery matches the details on the note.

Delivery note

Date 1/05/01
Order number 258
Our reference 6678
Your reference Y5551

To: Hatrick
Unit 5
Elmhurst Trading Estate
Southampton

From: A&B Textiles
123 Park Street
Bradford

Catalogue number	Quantity	Description
Y056	2	10m length yellow textile material
Checked by	Tim (warehouse)	Sign on delivery

A goods received note is made out by Hatrick and addressed to the supplier A&B Textiles. It records what has actually been delivered and is checked against the delivery note. Hatrick will keep a copy.

Goods received note

To: A&B Textiles
123 Park Street
Bradford

Date 1/05/01
Order number 258
Our reference Y5551
Your reference

From: Hatrick
Unit 5
Elmhurst Trading Estate
Southampton

Catalogue number	Quantity	Description
Y056	2	10m length yellow textile material
Received by	James Monro (warehouse – goods in department)	Date: 1/05/01

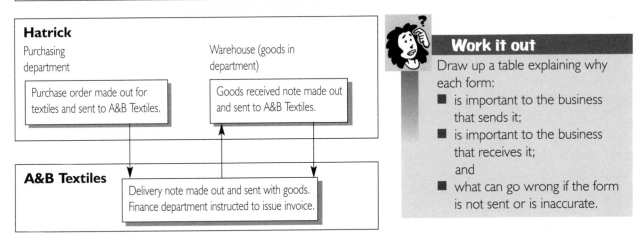

Hatrick

Purchasing department

Purchase order made out for textiles and sent to A&B Textiles.

Warehouse (goods in department)

Goods received note made out and sent to A&B Textiles.

A&B Textiles

Delivery note made out and sent with goods. Finance department instructed to issue invoice.

Work it out

Draw up a table explaining why each form:
- is important to the business that sends it;
- is important to the business that receives it; and
- what can go wrong if the form is not sent or is inaccurate.

Keeping the cash flowing

What's it all about?

You need to understand how each document contributes to the flow of financial information.

Invoice

Date 1/05/01
Order number 258
Invoice number 6678
Your reference Y5551

To: Hatrick
Unit 5, Elmhurst Trading Estate
Southampton

From: A&B Textiles
123 Park Street
Bradford

Catalogue number	Quantity	Description	Unit price	Total price
Y056	2	10m length yellow textile material	£89.00	£178.00
			Total	£178.00
			Less trade discount 10%	£160.20
			Add VAT at 17.5%	£28.03
				£188.23
			Postage (carriage)	£28.64
			Total	£216.87

Pay within 30 days   1% discount if paid within 7 days of invoice

When the supplier, A&B Textiles, sends a delivery note to the warehouse at Hatrick it also sends an invoice to the finance department at Hatrick.

The **invoice** is a bill to remind the customer what goods were bought and what needs to be paid. It also states when this needs to be paid. It is a legal agreement between the buyer and seller.

On receiving the invoice from A&B Textiles, Hatrick's finance department will check whether the goods have been delivered and checked by the warehouse. This is easily done if the recording system is on the computer. The finance department then has to pay the invoice at the agreed time. It can be paid by cheque.

This will show up on the **monthly bank statement** as a debit (money going out of the account). The bank statement can be checked against the cash book to ensure that all transactions are recorded and payments made. It will also show bank charges and interest payments which allow you to complete your records.

Work it out

Phil has to work out how to deal with the invoice.

1 How many days credit has A&B given Hatrick?

2 What is the trade discount? How much is the discount on this invoice?

3 How much will Phil save if the bill is paid quickly?

4 Why does A&B offer this encouragement for people to pay quickly?

5 How much does Hatrick owe A&B?

6 What date does Hatrick need to pay by?

Meanwhile, Hatrick has received a cheque and some cash from two customers and will deposit this with the bank by filling in a **paying in slip**. It will also show up on the bank statement, but this time as a credit (money coming into the account).

Bank statement

Title of account Hatrick current account

Branch number 15-1254

Account number 12358657

The Royal Bank plc
Southampton Branch

Date	Details	Debit (withdrawn)	Credit (paid in)	Balance
	Balance brought forward			£412.80
1/6/01	Paid in		£376.30	£789.10
2/6/01	Cheque number 9410	£216.87		£572.23

Work it out

1 What value would Hatrick make the cheque to A&B Textiles?

2 What would the value have been if Hatrick had paid the April statement of account in full?

3 What worries would A&B Textiles have about Hatrick? How does keeping records help them to decide about future deliveries?

If the business has regular orders with one supplier it may settle the accounts once a month when the suppliers send a **statement of account**.

Statement of account   **A&B Textiles**

To: Hatrick
Unit 5,
Elmhurst Trading Estate
Southampton

Hatrick didn't settle its bill in April. The sum is added on to the amount that is due in May. A&B Textiles will want a full payment.

123 Park Street, Bradford

Date: 29/5/01
Account number: Hat22
Reference: 56754

Date	Details	Debit	Credit	Balance
29/4/01	Previous balance			£405.78
7/5/01	Credit note Y45		£74.00	£331.78
28/5/01	Goods supplied on invoice 6678	£216.87		£548.65

A&B sent materials of the wrong colour and have given Hatrick a credit note.

Remittance advice

Date: 29/5/01
Account number: Hat22
Reference: 56754

Total due £548.65

The remittance advice will be torn off by Hatrick and sent with the payment.

This is what Hatrick owe A&B Textiles on 29/5/01.

A **remittance advice** is sent by the customer to the supplier with details of the invoices that have been paid at that time. A&B Textiles attaches a tear off slip to the statement of account it sends to Hatrick. Hatrick then returns the remittance advice with the payment.

Hatrick

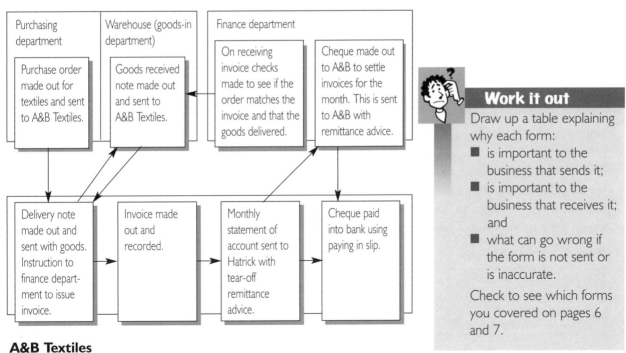

Work it out

Draw up a table explaining why each form:

■ is important to the business that sends it;

■ is important to the business that receives it; and

■ what can go wrong if the form is not sent or is inaccurate.

Check to see which forms you covered on pages 6 and 7.

A&B Textiles

Following the flow

What's it all about?

You need to understand the flow of accounting information between books of original entry and the personal and general ledgers.

Work it out

1 Why do you think most businesses use computers to run their finances?

2 Why is it important to understand how the information put into the computer is used and how it contributes to the final accounts of the business?

Many of the documents we have looked at, such as invoices and credit notes, are used to help make up the general accounts of the business. The information from these original, or source, documents must all be entered into **day books** (sometimes known as **journals**) and the information from these is transferred across to the **ledger**. This transfer might be done once a month if accounts are still completed by hand, or automatically if computers are used. The ledger contains all the financial entries for the business. The ledger is usually split into two main parts.

- Personal ledger
  - ○ Purchase ledger
  - ○ Sales ledger
- General ledger

The **personal ledger** contains the records of all transactions with individual customers and suppliers. It is divided into two parts. A business can immediately check in the **purchase ledger** to find out what it owes to each supplier and in the **sales ledger** to discover what is owed by each customer.

The **general ledger** shows every transaction that goes through the business, so it includes rent and wages for example. It also contains a summary of the information in the **personal ledger.**

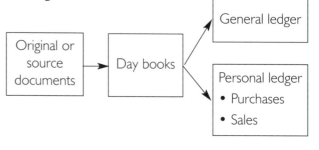

BUYING IN

When a business gets an invoice for items that it has bought from a supplier, it records the basic details in the **purchase day book**. A business might receive a credit note because it has returned faulty goods. The details of this are entered in the **returns outwards day book**.

The information from both day books is transferred to the **purchase ledger** and then the **general ledger**.

The **purchase ledger** has all the personal accounts of the credit suppliers of the business. Track the transactions through the following entries.

Purchase day book (journal)

Date	Details of suppliers	Invoice number	Total
19/5	Birdtex	38789	£159.06
29/5	A&B Textiles	6678	£216.87
		Totals for the month of May	**£375.93**

Returns outwards day book

Date	Credit note details	Credit note number	Total
7/5	A&B Textiles	Y45	£74.00
	Totals for the month of May		**£74.00**

Purchase ledger (suppliers' accounts)

A&B Textiles

Date	Details	Debit	Credit	Balance
7/5	Credit note Y45		£74.00	£142.87
29/5	Invoice 6678	£216.87		£216.87

Birdtex

Date	Details	Debit	Credit	Balance
19/5		£159.06		£159.06

SELLING PRODUCTS

When a business sends out an invoice after a sale has been made, the basic details are written in the **sales day book**. If this business sends out a credit note the details are recorded in the **returns inwards day book**. The information from both day books is transferred to the **sales ledger** and then to the **general ledger**. The sales ledger has all the personal accounts of customers of the business. Track the transactions through the following entries.

Sales day book (journal)

Date	Details	Invoice number	Total
15/5	Hats R Us	3456	£90.45
17/5	Clothes Unlimited	3457	£216.87
29/5	Hats R Us	3458	£68.98
		Total	**£376.30**

Returns inwards day book

Date	Credit note details	Credit note number	Total
29/5	Clothes Unlimited	B465	£10.50
		Total	**£10.50**

Sales ledger (customer accounts)

Hats R Us

Date	Details	Debit	Credit	Balance
15/5	Goods invoice 3456	£90.45		£90.45
29/5	Goods invoice 3458	£68.98		£159.43

Clothes unlimited

Date	Details	Debit	Credit	Balance
17/5	Goods invoice 3457	£216.87		£216.87
29/5	Credit note B465		£10.50	£206.37

PUTTING IT ALL TOGETHER

The general ledger contains information from the purchase ledger, the sales ledger and any other transactions, e.g. paying the rent.

General ledger

Date	Monthly total	Debit	Credit
31/5	Sales		£376.30
	Returns inwards	£10.50	
	Purchases	£375.93	
	Returns outwards		£74.00
	Rent	£550	

Work it out

1 Why is the personal ledger important to a business?

2 Why is it important to be able to track transactions?

3 If you want an overall picture of the finances of a business, where do you look?

Cheques and double checks

What's it all about?

You need to understand the management of these documents and explain their use and importance for stakeholders.

(a) I ordered 2 times 10m lengths of textile materials not 10 lots.

(b) Our customer has only paid us £200.50 instead of £2005.00.

(c) They ordered 50 hats, but we delivered 10.

(d) They have delivered 20 hats and only charged for 2.

(e) Who gave permission to buy that much material? It will last us a year.

(f) Well, this lot of textiles we bought are the wrong colour.

(g) They say we gave them 60 days' credit.

SORTING IT OUT

From: Hatrick
To: A&B Textiles
Date: 1/5/01
Our purchase order form number 339032 dated 17/4/01 shows that we placed an order for yellow textile rolls, but on opening them we note that two rolls are a deep red colour. I checked our stock levels and we can do without the rolls for a while. Please collect the red textiles when you next deliver. In the meantime I hope you can give us a credit note (invoice reference 289-54).
Jessie Jones
Purchasing manager

A **credit note** gives details of the amount of credit given when a customer returns faulty goods or has accidentally been overcharged. The customer will then pay less in the next bill to the value of the credit note. Look at 'What's gone wrong' to find some examples.

Work it out

1 Identify which documents you would need to check against for each of the above examples.

2 For each situation suggest what you could you do to make it less likely to happen again in the future.

3 What can you do about each to put it right now?

A credit note may be issued by the supplier A&B Textiles for (a) and (f). Hatrick might issue a credit note for (c) if their invoice was for 50 hats.

Credit note			**A&B Textiles**	
To Hatrick Unit 5 Elmhurst Trading Estate Southampton			123 Park Street Bradford Credit note number Y45 Invoice number 289-54 Date 3/5//01	
Quantity	Description		Unit price	Price
2	10m lengths of material (sent wrong colour)		£37	£74
			Total	£74

WHAT'S WRONG WITH ERRORS?

Keeping accurate records makes it less likely that the business will make errors and this will save the business time and money. The fewer the errors the better the reputation of the business, which means it will be trusted by others.

Keeping accurate records also means you are more likely to spot any errors quickly and be able to correct them. Remember errors can be from the businesses you deal with (external errors) or from within your own business (internal errors).

Having a clear financial system helps a business keep accurate records and makes sure employees don't do things they shouldn't. The bigger the business the more specialist the employees are. In a large business there will be separate departments to deal with orders or purchases, delivery, sales records, paying bills and general accounts. Within these departments, employees will have their own area of responsibility. Some documents need to be authorised before they can be sent off. For example, large orders must be signed by someone in management with the authority to say the money can be spent. Cheques need to be countersigned to ensure they are correct.

Getting things wrong has its costs.

Every time someone has to spend time unpicking the mess, it is time wasted. The job adverts below suggest that you don't want to be employing more people in the finance department than is absolutely necessary.

A business that keeps getting things wrong develops a poor reputation with both suppliers and customers. If the paper work is unpredictable, people may decide to look for alternatives. Staff are also affected because they expect to be paid promptly and accurately. Unhappy **stakeholders** are bad for business.

ACCOUNTS PAYABLE CONTROLLER

£16–18K + bonus + benefits

You will manage processing of invoices, payments to suppliers and maintenance of the purchase ledger. You will report to the financial controller.

Two years' experience is required.

Accounts Receivable Controller

£16–18K + bonus + benefits

You will manage the receivable operation of the business and will report to the financial controller. Your duties include debt collection, maintenance of the sales ledger and the setting and application of credit limits.

Two years' experience is required.

Work it out

1 Draw up a flow diagram to track the records when an order is placed.

2 Draw up a flow diagram to track the records when a sale is returned.

3 Draw a spider diagram with 'When things go wrong' at the centre. Identify all the problems that arise as a result of things going wrong. How can they be overcome?

Testing times: AQA

The following questions are adapted from AQA tests.

Assessment evidence	
E1	Identify why businesses need to keep accurate financial records
E3	Identify the links between financial documents and how financial information flows through the accounting system
C1	Explain the consequences of inaccurate record keeping
C3	Explain the links between financial documents and how financial information flows through the accounting system
A1	Evaluate the consequences of inaccurate recording of financial data

Mouncey Ltd makes components for mobile telephones. The manager of the accounts department has just appointed a junior clerk. As part of the training for the new employee, the manager explains the importance of keeping accurate financial records and major documents used by the business.

Mouncey Ltd received an order from a new customer, Eagle Communications plc, for 25 000 circuit boards at £2.50 each less a trade discount of 5%. The goods were subject to VAT at the standard rate of 17.5%.

The new clerk was given responsibility for issuing the invoice. A week later the manager of the accounts department received a complaint from Eagle Communications plc, that they had not been given the discount.

Ordering and delivering
page 6 tells you about the paper work that tracks the goods.

Keeping the cash flowing
page 8 has information about the financial documents.

1 **Complete the flow chart by writing the name of the correct financial documents that should be in each of the numbered boxes.** **5 marks**

Assessment evidence: E3

 This question requires knowledge of the flow of documents between businesses. You also need to be sure that you understand the purpose of each document.

Answer

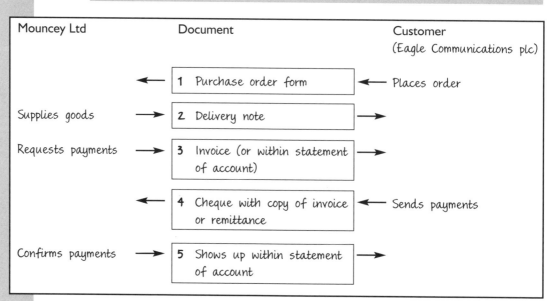

2 Calculate the correct value of the invoice that the new clerk should have sent to Eagle Communications plc.   **5 marks**

Assessment evidence: E1

Help! This question asks you to apply number by showing how a discount is worked out.

Answer

25 000 x £2.50 = £62 500 without discount.
Discount at 5% = £62 500 x .05 = £3125.
Actual invoice should be £62 500 − £3125 = £59 375.

Keeping the cash flowing
page 8 demonstrates a discount.

3 Explain how Mouncey Ltd might correct an error in an invoice they have issued.   **3 marks**

Assessment evidence: E1, E3, C3

Help! You need to know the process, be able to use it as well as being aware of the effect of an error.

Answer

The normal method is to issue a credit note for the amount Mouncey overcharged its customer. Mouncey will record the credit note in the sales returns day book. The customer will set it off against the next purchase made. However, Eagle Communications plc is a new customer and if this was a one off order a cheque would need to be sent.

Keeping the cash flowing
page 8 explains the documents and the process.

Following the flow
page 11 tracks a credit note through day books.

Cheques and double checks
page 12 explains the effect of an error.

4 Explain two possible consequences to Mouncey Ltd of issuing incorrect invoices.   **6 marks**

Assessment evidence: C1, A1

Help! The question asks for **2** consequences so give 2. There are no more marks for more than 2. One consequence will only get half marks. Any question that will give you an A is looking for evaluation. You need to think about the effects on two stakeholders, either within or outside the business. Draw a quick flow diagram showing the impact to help you think.

Answer

Customers will be annoyed by mistakes. If the mistakes are common then the customers feel they are not getting a good service and may decide to take their business elsewhere. Eagle Communications plc is a new customer and will be left with a bad impression of Mouncey Ltd. It is important to build trust between the buyer and seller.

Mistakes take time and effort to sort out. It means that the work has to be done twice over. The staff who have to put things right are being paid. This is a cost to the business and a sign of inefficiency.

Mistakes could be minimised if Mouncey Ltd. kept a log of mistakes and then took action to reduce them by improving their training for staff. A reduction in errors will save money in the long term and keep customers and suppliers happy.

Cheques and double checks
page 12 provides a range of examples of the consequences of the invoice being wrong. The first section, in general, also uses things going wrong as a way of explaining how the documents and ledgers are used.

Testing times: Edexcel

The following questions are adapted from Edexcel tests.

Assessment evidence	
EI	Identify why businesses need to keep accurate financial records
E3	Identify the links between financial documents and how financial information flows through the accounting system
CI	Explain the consequences of inaccurate record keeping
C3	Explain the links between financial documents and how financial information flows through the accounting system
AI	Evaluate the consequences of inaccurate recording of financial data

1 **An invoice is received by R Dobi from a supplier Elbee Ltd. Select from the list below the correct book or account which would show how this invoice would flow through the accounting system. Complete the shaded boxes.** **3 marks**

- **Creditor account**
- **Debtor account**
- **Purchase day book**
- **Sales day book**
- **Sales account**
- **Purchase account**
- **Not entered**

Assessment evidence: E3

Keeping the cash flowing
page 8 for information about the financial documents.

Help! This question requires knowledge of the flow of documents and information through a business. It is useful to understand why the information flows as it does because it helps you to remember.

Answer

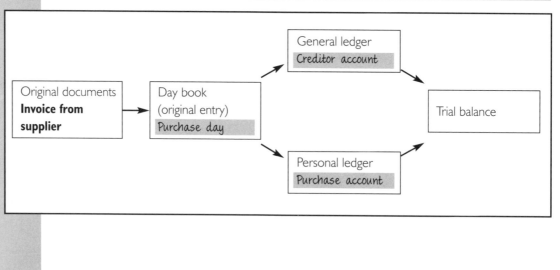

2 State why Dobi enters this transaction in the personal ledger.

2 marks

Assessment evidence: C3

Help! To answer this question you need to be able to explain the purpose of the personal ledger.

Answer

The personal ledger records all the personal accounts of credit suppliers to Dobi. There will be one account for the supplier Elbee Ltd. It is easy to check on the business dealings with Elbee Ltd because all the details can be found in one account.

Following the flow page 10 explains the purpose of the documents and how they work together.

3 Dobi has received a statement from its bank. Explain fully how Dobi should use the bank statement as a checking tool.

3 marks

Assessment evidence: C3

Help! This question is looking at the checking mechanisms in the system. By double checking, greater accuracy is ensured.

Answer

Dobi should check the bank statement against the cash book entries. The cash book will record payments of invoices or the statements of accounts as well as cash payments. The cash book also lists deposits, which are payments to the business from others. As the statement includes all monies received and paid from the bank account, gaps can be filled. It will include, for example, interest payments and charges by the bank as well as any regular payments.

Keeping the cash flowing page 8 explains how the bank statement is used to check the records.

4 In each case below consider the accounting flows and state the revised net profit if the error is corrected.

2 marks

Assessment evidence: E1, C1

Help! To answer this you need to understand the role of the books and ledgers in the system. When things have gone wrong, this relationship is important because it helps you to track the source of the problem.

Ordering and delivering page 6 explains entries in the cash book.
Following the flow page 10 explains the role of the personal ledger.

Answer

Original net profit	Error	Revised net profit
(a) £9000	Purchase of stock costing £1000 had been recorded as a sale of stock	£7000
(b) £19 000	A sale of stock for £600 to J Brown had been recorded into the account of P Browne	£19 000

Cheques and double checks
page 12 looks at customers
as stakeholders.

How profitable is it? page 48
explains profit margin.

What's the return? Page 54
explains ROCE.

5 In each case evaluate the consequences to the business of not correcting the error.

4 marks

Assessment evidence: A1

Help! This question is somewhat unrealistic. Double entry book keeping should avoid these problems. If the cheque is wrongly recorded, the trial balance wouldn't balance and the source of the problem would have to be found. The second problem would be discovered when the personal ledgers were checked. However, on a theoretical basis, the following answers stand.

Answer

In case (a) the final accounts would not show the true performance of the business with the net profit being smaller than that stated. This would exaggerate the performance ratios such as net profit margin and ROCE.

In case (b) the revised net profit is the same as the sale that has been made, but it is recorded to the wrong personal sales ledger. However, if statements of account are drawn from this ledger J Brown will have been undercharged and P Browne overcharged. P Browne would complain and a credit note would be issued. Inaccurate financial transactions may affect the attitude of customers, who are important stakeholders in the business.

6 Complete the shaded boxes on the invoice.

4 marks

Assessment evidence: E3

Help! This question asks you to make some calculations and to show that you understand trade discount. Check your calculations carefully.

Keeping the cash flowing
page 8 shows you how to
complete an invoice and
apply a discount.

Answer

Invoice		To:		From:	
Date 1/06/01		Armicom		East Computer Supplies	
		5 High St		38 Clift Park	
Invoice number 6678					
Your reference Y5551					

	Quantity	Description		Unit price	Total price
	2	desk		£38.72	£77.44
	1	video recorder		£285.00	£285.00
	3	14" television		£125.32	£375.96
				Total	£738.40
				Trade discount 25%	£184.60
				Subtotal	£553.80
				+ VAT at 17.5%	£96.92
				Total	£650.72

Pay within 28 days   1.25% discount if paid within 14 days of invoice

7 How much should Armicom pay if they <u>do not</u> settle the
invoice within 14 days.

1 mark

Assessment evidence: E1, E3

Keeping the cash flowing
page 8 shows you how to
interpret an invoice.

Help! If part of a question is underlined, look carefully. It is usually trying to stop you
falling into a trap. In this case, the answer is easy. The number of marks available
should be a clue.

Answer

£650.72 because Armicom do not qualify for the extra 1.25% discount.

---

8 By referring to three named documents linked to this invoice,
explain what information should be checked by Armicom
before payment is made.

3 marks

Assessment evidence: E3, C3

Ordering and delivering
page 6 explains the paper
work which tracks the flow of
goods.

Help! This question looks at tracking the flow of goods against the financial records. It
is a logical process so think in terms of a flow diagram to help remember it.

Answer

*Armicom would need to know if the goods had been ordered so it
would need to check on the purchase order form. It would need to
know if the goods had been delivered and had been checked against
the delivery note and invoice. Armicom would also check its copy of
the goods received note.*

Testing times: OCR

The following questions are adapted from OCR tests. OCR uses a case study approach. An extract is given below.

Assessment evidence	
E1	Identify why businesses need to keep accurate financial records
E2	Identify different stakeholders and explain their interests in gaining financial information about the business
C1	Explain the consequences of inaccurate record keeping
A1	Evaluate the consequences of inaccurate recording of financial data

Keeping the cash flowing
page 8 explains the importance of documents and records that track the flow of money.

Following the flow page 10 explains the importance of documents and records which track the flow of goods.

Building a budget page 76 explains the information needed to put a budget together.

... and forecasting cash flow
page 78 explains the information needed to look at cash flow.

Cheques and double checks
page 12 shows the effects of errors on customers and suppliers.

INFORMAL REPORT by Sam Hopkinson (newly appointed finance and administration manager)

1 INTRODUCTION

There are a number of issues relating to the financial system, operated by CD Productions Ltd, that need to be addressed.

2 FINDINGS

The main problem areas are:

- Any money in the bank or held on site is being used by the first person to need it with no thought or concern for the needs of others later on.
- Quotes, orders and cheques are piling up as there is no system for these to be dealt with.
- Invoices from suppliers and utility providers are very late in being paid. Two letters threatening legal action have already been received.
- Financial record keeping to date is disorganised and incomplete.
- Accurate final accounts will have to be produced by law at the end of the year and lodged with Companies House.

All of these problem areas can be dealt with effectively by introducing new systems and allocating specific roles and responsibilities to staff.

---

1 **Identify four reasons why Sam felt it important to set up a new system to record financial information.** **4 marks**

Assessment evidence: E1, E2

Help! You need a range of knowledge to select the problems which Sam identified. It is straightforward but make sure that you can link them to question 2. A quick spider diagram would give you the answer to both questions as you can see the links.

Answer

Select from:
There is no control of the budget.
There is no order to processing quotes and orders and cheques.
The business is in danger of losing its credit reputation.
No one knows how well the business is doing in financial terms.
The business is not in a position to produce accurate accounts to be sent to Companies House.

2 Explain the possible consequences for CD Productions Ltd
if improvements are not made to their financial record
keeping.   **4 marks**

Assessment evidence: E2, C1

> **Help!** What a mess! The business won't last long if it goes on like this. This follows
> from the previous question and asks you to consider the implications. The pages
> identified above will help you.

Answer

The business may run out of cash as there is no control of the
budget.
Orders may be lost because they are not dealt with efficiently.
Suppliers may refuse to do business if CD Productions Ltd fails to pay
bills.
Cheques are not quickly put into the bank meaning the bank balance is
lower than it should be.
The business may be in an unhealthy financial state, but no one is
monitoring it. It is impossible to plan the future without knowledge of
the current state of play.

---

3 CD Productions Ltd had no managers with financial expertise until
they appointed Sam. One of the directors, Stella, had previously
commented that the business was in danger of collapse.
To what extent could her comments be true?
Justify your answer.   **6 marks**

Assessment evidence: A1

> **Help!** Stella had obviously got some grasp of how a business works, even if she had
> not got the financial expertise to deal with the problems. You need to look at
> the problems and evaluate their significance as a source of potential crisis.

Answer

The company is getting both the tracking of goods and money wrong. If
it continues it will destroy relationships with both customers and
suppliers. This will remove the purpose of the business as all the
stakeholders will become disenchanted and go elsewhere.
In financial terms, unless the business sorts out its financial
monitoring it is likely to become insolvent because its cash flow is out
of control. The money may be there but is unavailable to pay bills as
cheques have not been paid into the bank. Eventually the creditors will
take legal action which may result in the business going into
liquidation.
If the business is unable to produce annual accounts, it will be fined
initially but, in the longer term, be unable to trade as its company
registration will be withdrawn.

Testing times: practice questions

1 Why should all orders be authorised?

2 A cheque is wrongly made out to a supplier for £500 when the value of the goods delivered was £600. If nothing was done, which accounts would incorrectly show higher profits and which would show lower profits?

3 If the supplier spotted the mistake and contacted the credit customer what would happen next?

4 What might happen if the credit customer frequently made out cheques to the wrong value?

5 How might the credit customer reduce errors?

6 What do you understand by a source document?

7 Which of these are source documents?

- Sales ledger
- Invoice
- Trial balance
- Credit note

8 Why would credit customers wait for regular suppliers to send a statement of account before settling invoices? State the advantages for each business.

---

9 Complete these forms by filling in the grey boxes.

Purchase order form				From: Hatrick
To: A&B Textiles		Date 23/07/01		Unit 5
123 Park Street		Order number 258		Elmhurst Trading Estate
Bradford		Our reference Y55-0-1		Southampton

Catalogue number	Quantity	Description	Unit price	Total
Y550	5	Boxes of black thread		£20
Y551	3	Boxes of red thread	£5	
			Total	

Delivery date 11/08/01

Signed
Authorised by

Delivery note		To: Hatrick	From: A&B Textiles
Date 11/08/01		Unit 5	123 Park Street
Order number 258		Elmhurst Trading Estate	Bradford
Our reference 6678		Southampton	
Your reference Y55-0-1			

Catalogue number	Quantity	Description
Y550	5	Boxes of
		Boxes of red thread

Checked by Tim (warehouse)

Sign on delivery

Goods received note		Date 11/08/01	From: Hatrick
To: A&B Textiles		Order number 258	Unit 5
123 Park Street		Our reference Y55-0-1	Elmhurst Trading Estate
Bradford		Your reference	Southampton

Catalogue number	Quantity	Description	

Received by James Munro (warehouse – goods-in department)
Date 11/08/01

10 The accounts receivable clerk for Muddy Mountain Bikes opens the post at various days during the week to find three remittance advice notes with cheques for the sale of its bikes to shops.

15/5 Avon Valley Bikes Shop 10 bikes total cheque value £2000
15/5 Bikes R Us   5 bikes total cheque value £1000
19/5 Bikes R Us   20 bikes total cheque value £4000

A fax arrived on 19/5 from Avon Valley Bikes Shop stating two of the bikes they had ordered were the wrong colour and have been sent back.

Complete the documents below assuming these are new customers.

Sales day book (journal)

Date	Details	Invoice number	Total
15/5			
		Total	

Returns inwards day book

Date	Credit note details	Credit note number	Total
		Total	£400

Sales ledger (customer accounts)

Avon Valley Bikes Shop

Date	Details	Debit	Credit	Balance

Bikes R Us

Date	Details	Debit	Credit	Balance

General ledger

Date	Monthly total	Debit	Credit
19/05	Sales		
19/05	Returns inwards		
19/05	Purchases	£1200	
19/05	Returns outwards		£90.00

11 What ledger was used to obtain the sum of the purchases of stock for Muddy Mountain Bikes?

12 What ledger was used to obtain the credit value of £90?

From ledgers to final accounts

> 'Keeping all those records pays off in the end!'

What's it all about?

You need to understand how information from the general ledger is used to produce the trial balance, and information from the trial balance is used to construct the balance sheet and profit and loss account.

Work it out

1 Why does keeping careful records help?
2 Track the information from source documents to the general ledger.
3 What is the advantage of everything having to balance at every stage?

CREATING A TRIAL BALANCE

The day books and ledgers are the record keeping process. The summary of all the balances from the various ledgers becomes the trial balance. For example the money received from all sales may be grouped together. Costs would also be grouped together. For example, all the material purchases would be added up and entered as the sum value. The same would apply for the rent and for the salaries. The debit section of the trial balance will match the credit section unless something has gone wrong. All the information in the trial balance will be split into either the profit and loss account or the balance sheet. These are called the final accounts and are used to assess how well the business has performed.

The **profit and loss account** is drawn up from entries into the trial balance that are to do with business costs and revenues (turnover) from sales. The profit and loss account shows how much profit or loss a business has made over a period of time, known as the accounting period. This is usually six months or one year.

The **balance sheet** is all to do with where the finance comes from (sources of finance) and how it is used (uses of finance). Money will be used to buy assets. It is a freeze frame of the business at the time it is drawn up.

JO'S TRIAL BALANCE

Jo's Diner is a converted old coach parked in a field close to her house and near a layby of a busy country road. Jo and her staff serve meals all day.

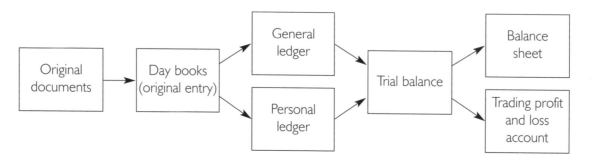

Original documents → Day books (original entry) → General ledger / Personal ledger → Trial balance → Balance sheet / Trading profit and loss account

Trial balance for Jo's Diner at 30 April 2001 (after a year of trading)

What the account covers	Account	Debit	Credit
Turnover from sales (sales revenue).	Sales		110000
Materials bought from suppliers	Purchases	62000	
Value of stock at start of trading year	Stock at 1.5.2000	Nil	
Expense	Insurance	6000	
Expense	Depreciation	4000	
Includes salaries	Other expenses	33900	
These are fixed assets. The business owns them. Every year their value will change. The value of most fixed assets fall (depreciate). The current value must be assessed and is called the **net book value**.	Computer equipment	2000	
	Equipment	5000	
	Coach and fittings	31000	
Business customers who still owe Jo's Diner money.	Debtors	9000	
Businesses, usually suppliers, that Jo's Diner still owes money to.	Creditors		5500
The money balance held in Jo's Diner's bank account.	Bank	3500	
How much cash Jo's Diner holds.	Cash	1000	
The value of the investment by the owners of the business.	Capital at 30 April 2001		24000
Money lent by the bank or other backer.	Long term loan		23000
Money earned from deposits.	Interest received		150
Money paid on borrowing.	Interest paid	1250	
Resources, like money, withdrawn from the business by the owner.	Drawings	4000	
The credit and debit columns must **balance**.	Total	**162650**	**162650**

FOLLOW THE FLOW

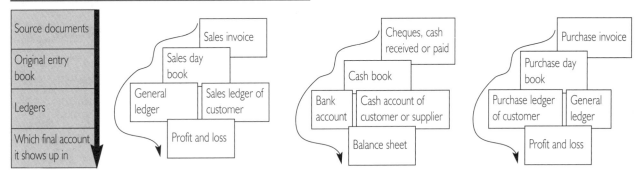

Work it out

1 Identify which entries from Jo's Diner's trial balance will be used to draw up the profit and loss account and which will be used for the balance sheet.

Jo wanted to buy better equipment such as freezers and a dishwasher that used little water. She also wanted outside furniture for the summer.

Jo found a partner to invest another £5000 in the business. Assume it is now 1 May 2001.

2 How would the trial balance change on the credit side?

3 How would this now change the debit side?

4 When she purchased her equipment what would happen to the debit side?

5 What original documents would she get from the suppliers?

6 Into which day book would she enter the information from the documents?

Is the balance right?

What's it all about?

You need to understand how a simple balance sheet is constructed and be able to distinguish between assets and liabilities.

Jo had always wanted to run her own business but finding the right premises was an expensive proposition. Then she came up with the bright idea of converting a coach. This meant she could go to the market instead of the market coming to her.

In order to borrow money from the bank, she had to have a clear picture of where the money would come from and what she would use it for. The **balance sheet** does just this so she had to think about what would happen when the business was under way.

WHAT DOES A BALANCE SHEET DO?

The balance sheet records where the money comes from to finance the business (sources of finance) and how it is used (uses of finance).

As you might guess, it has two sections. One shows the **assets** – or the business's possessions:

■ **fixed assets** are items that are not intended for resale;

■ **current assets** are assets that can be turned into cash in the near future. This includes stock and money that is owed by debtors or customers as well as bank deposits.

The other section shows the **liabilities** – or the business's debts:

■ **long term liabilities** do not need to be paid back within at least twelve months of the balance sheet date, e.g. a bank loan;

■ **current liabilities** need to be paid back within twelve months, e.g. payments to suppliers, or creditors and bank overdrafts.

Work it out

When Jo set up in business as Jo's Diner, she bought and converted an old coach into a diner with a kitchen, bar and eating area.

1 What did she have to buy to get her Diner going?

2 What would she need to run the business side?

3 Why would she need to keep some cash in the bank?

4 Where do you think the money came from?

JO'S BALANCE SHEET

Jo bought all the things she needed to get the business underway. She kept back some cash so she could keep the business running. A computer and colour printer meant that she could organise her accounts and produce menus and flyers.

She paid for most of her purchases herself from her savings. This is called the capital. She arranged a bank loan for the rest of the money she needed.

Work it out

1 Make one list of Jo's fixed assets and another for her current assets once the business is running.

2 Do the same for her long term and current liabilities.

3 What is likely to happen if the liabilities are greater than the assets?

CONSTRUCTING ACCOUNTS

This is what her balance sheet meant.

Where the finance comes from	How the finance is used
Bank loan	Cash and bank balance
	Stocks
Owner's capital	Computer
	Equipment
	Coach

At the end of the first year, her balance sheet looked like this. It has been drawn up from her ledgers on the computer system.

Jo's Diner balance sheet dated 30 April 2001

Use of funds			
Fixed assets			
Computer	2000		
Coach	31 000		
Equipment	5000		
		38 000	
Current assets			
Stock	10 000		
Debtors	9000		
Bank	3500		
Cash	1000		
		23 500	
Current liabilities			
Creditors	(5500)		
		(5500)	
Working capital		18 000	
Net assets		56 000	
Financed by			
Capital	24 000		
Profits	13 000		
Drawings	(4000)		
		33 000	
Long term liabilities			
Long term loan		23 000	
Net worth		56 000	

This column is for the calculations.

This column is for the main totals.

This column is for subtotals.

Brackets show something which is to be deducted.

Net assets are made up of fixed assets and working capital.

Working capital is made up of current assets minus current liabilities.

ANOTHER WAY OF LOOKING AT IT

Public companies have to show how shareholders' money is being used. To do this, long term liabilities are excluded as they will have to be paid back eventually.

Some accounts set out the balance sheet like this.

Assets		
Fixed assets		38 000
Working capital		18 000
		56 000
Long term liabilities		
Long term loan		(23 000)
Net assets		33 000
Financed by		
Capital	24 000	
Profits	13 000	
Drawings	(4000)	
Net worth		33 000

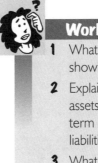

Work it out

1 What does a balance sheet show?

2 Explain the meaning of fixed assets, current assets, long term liabilities and current liabilities.

3 What is working capital and how is it worked out?

4 Why is the net worth of Jo's Diner shown differently from the net worth of a public company?

Staying in balance

What's it all about?

You need to understand how a simple balance sheet is constructed and be able to distinguish between assets and liabilities.

Work it out

1. Why is Jo dreaming about buying tables and chairs for her diner?
2. Where might she raise the money to buy them?
3. What effect would raising the money and buying the chairs have on her balance sheet?

MOVING ON

Balance sheets balance because they have been set up to do so. If you borrow money, you have more liabilities but your assets increase when it goes into your bank account.

When you spend the money you've borrowed on new assets such as tables and chairs, it shifts from the bank balance box to the equipment box. Track the changes from Jo's balance sheet on the previous page through the following stages.

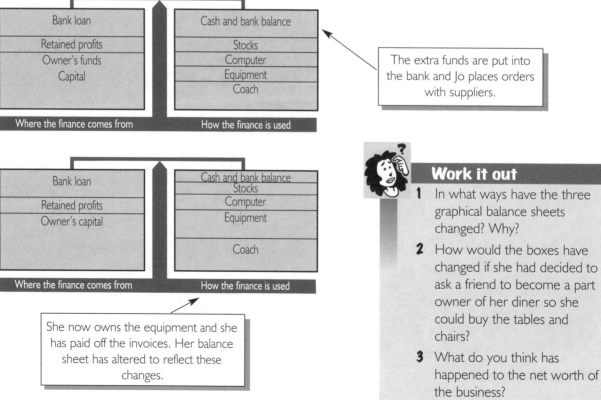

Bank loan	Cash and bank balance
Retained profits	Stocks
Owner's funds	Computer
Capital	Equipment
	Coach
Where the finance comes from	How the finance is used

The extra funds are put into the bank and Jo places orders with suppliers.

Bank loan	Cash and bank balance
	Stocks
Retained profits	Computer
Owner's capital	Equipment
	Coach
Where the finance comes from	How the finance is used

She now owns the equipment and she has paid off the invoices. Her balance sheet has altered to reflect these changes.

Work it out

1. In what ways have the three graphical balance sheets changed? Why?
2. How would the boxes have changed if she had decided to ask a friend to become a part owner of her diner so she could buy the tables and chairs?
3. What do you think has happened to the net worth of the business?

The balance sheet should balance because of the double entry system. Every time something is entered on the liabilities side, there will be a matching entry on the assets side.

For example, Jo decides to buy some new equipment for £3000. First, she gets a short-term loan to be paid back over the next year. Her current liabilities and her bank balance both rise by £3000. Then she buys the equipment. Her fixed assets rise by £3000 and her bank balance falls by £3000. She now has £3000 more fixed assets and £3000 more current liabilities than before. At every stage, there is a double entry as each transaction show up on both sides.

Jo has succeeded in winning a contract to supply a local business, Priddy's, with meals for its staff at lunchtime. She has few debtors for the Diner but she must keep an eye on the flow of payments from Priddy's to make sure that they are paying up regularly.

Jo's Diner balance sheet dated 30 April 2002

Use of funds		
Fixed assets		
Computer	2000	
Coach	31 000	
Equipment	8000	
		41 000
Current assets		
Stock	10 000	
Debtors	9000	
Bank	3500	
Cash	1000	
		23 500
Current liabilities		
Creditors	(8500) ◄	
		(8500)
Working capital		**15 000**
Net assets		**56 000**
Financed by		
Capital	24 000	
Profits	13 000	
Drawings	(4000)	
		33 000
Long term liabilities		
Long term loan		23 000
Net worth		**56 000**

This figure includes the short term loan of £3000.

Work it out

How will the balance sheet alter if Jo decides:
■ to reduce stocks by getting suppliers to deliver more frequently;
■ to buy a scanner with her own money;
■ to increase her drawings;
■ to chase up some debtors?

Work it out

Nick and Lucy run a business which develops websites for small organisations. They have:
■ a computer worth £2000;
■ a car, worth £6000, for visiting clients;
■ office equipment worth £1500;
■ stocks of materials worth £500;
■ £500 in cash;
■ £2500 in the bank.
They are owed £2500 by clients.
They owe £750 to suppliers.

They have taken £5000 out of the business as drawings.
To start the business, they put up £3000 between them.
Profits came to £9250.
The bank loan is £7500.
They love creating websites but hate accounts, so please draw up a balance sheet for their business.
When you've finished, can you give them any help to improve the situation?

What's the profit?

What's it all about?

You need to know how to construct a simple profit and loss account and be able to distinguish between revenues and expenses.

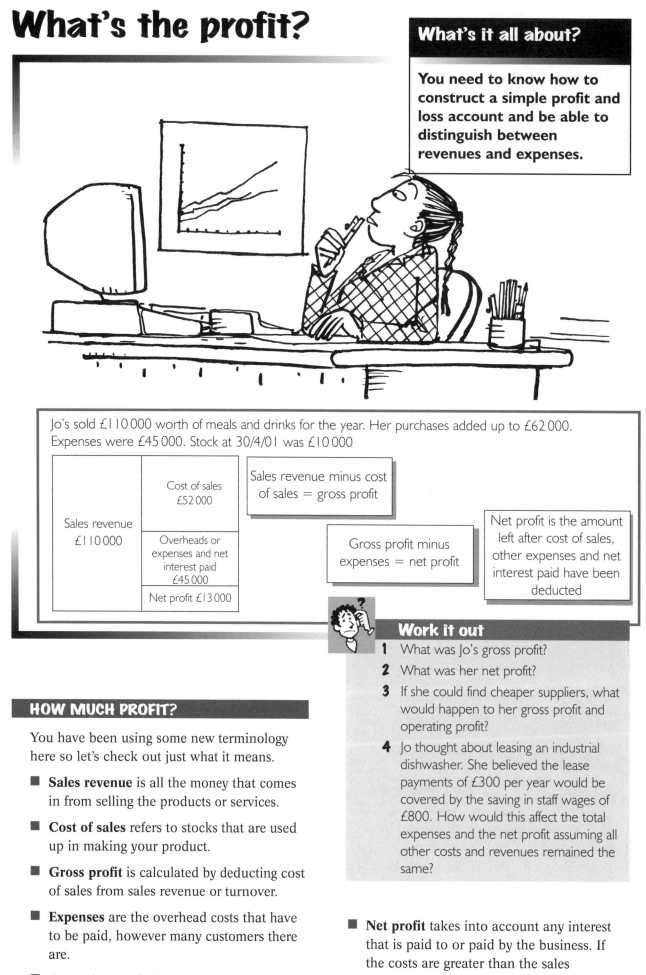

Jo's sold £110 000 worth of meals and drinks for the year. Her purchases added up to £62 000. Expenses were £45 000. Stock at 30/4/01 was £10 000

Sales revenue £110 000	Cost of sales £52 000
	Overheads or expenses and net interest paid £45 000
	Net profit £13 000

Sales revenue minus cost of sales = gross profit

Gross profit minus expenses = net profit

Net profit is the amount left after cost of sales, other expenses and net interest paid have been deducted

Work it out

1 What was Jo's gross profit?

2 What was her net profit?

3 If she could find cheaper suppliers, what would happen to her gross profit and operating profit?

4 Jo thought about leasing an industrial dishwasher. She believed the lease payments of £300 per year would be covered by the saving in staff wages of £800. How would this affect the total expenses and the net profit assuming all other costs and revenues remained the same?

HOW MUCH PROFIT?

You have been using some new terminology here so let's check out just what it means.

■ **Sales revenue** is all the money that comes in from selling the products or services.

■ **Cost of sales** refers to stocks that are used up in making your product.

■ **Gross profit** is calculated by deducting cost of sales from sales revenue or turnover.

■ **Expenses** are the overhead costs that have to be paid, however many customers there are.

■ **Operating profit** is the result of deducting expenses from gross profit.

■ **Net profit** takes into account any interest that is paid to or paid by the business. If the costs are greater than the sales revenue the business will have made a loss for that accounting period.

Look at Jo's Diner's profit and loss account.

Jo's Diner profit and loss account year ending 30 April 2001

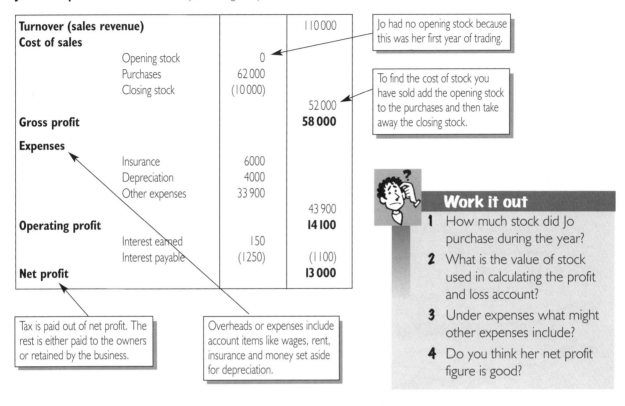

Turnover (sales revenue)		110 000
Cost of sales		
Opening stock	0	
Purchases	62 000	
Closing stock	(10 000)	
		52 000
Gross profit		**58 000**
Expenses		
Insurance	6000	
Depreciation	4000	
Other expenses	33 900	
		43 900
Operating profit		**14 100**
Interest earned	150	
Interest payable	(1250)	(1100)
Net profit		**13 000**

Jo had no opening stock because this was her first year of trading.

To find the cost of stock you have sold add the opening stock to the purchases and then take away the closing stock.

Tax is paid out of net profit. The rest is either paid to the owners or retained by the business.

Overheads or expenses include account items like wages, rent, insurance and money set aside for depreciation.

Work it out

1 How much stock did Jo purchase during the year?

2 What is the value of stock used in calculating the profit and loss account?

3 Under expenses what might other expenses include?

4 Do you think her net profit figure is good?

WHAT HAPPENS TO NET PROFIT?

■ **Paying taxes**

Companies pay **corporation tax** on their profits. It is collected by the Inland Revenue for the government.

■ **Paying the owners**

Sole traders and partners take **drawings** from the business. Shareholders in a company, both private and public, receive a **dividend**.

■ **Keeping it in the business**

The **retained profit** is kept in the business to be used for more fixed assets or to increase the working capital.

This is all shown in the **appropriation account**. This account shows what happens to the profit of a business.

Retained profit provides a link between the balance sheet and the profit and loss account. It is kept back by the business and becomes a source of funding just like issuing and selling

shares. The business's net worth, and therefore also the net assets, would increase by the value of the retained profits. The example assumes that there is no corporation tax and all the net profit is retained by the business.

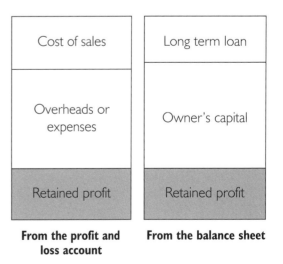

Cost of sales	Long term loan
Overheads or expenses	Owner's capital
Retained profit	Retained profit
From the profit and loss account	**From the balance sheet**

Wear and tear

What's it all about?

You need to know about depreciation and how it is calculated. You should also know the main factors that cause depreciation such as wear and tear, obsolescence and lack of maintenance.

HOW DO I ACCOUNT FOR IT?

When a business buys a new computer, dishwasher, or anything else that has a longish lifespan, it appears as an asset in the balance sheet. The net worth of the business doesn't change because cash or money in the bank has been used to pay for it.

If you look at a trial balance, it would be known as a balance sheet item.

What about the profit and loss account?

Many items that are bought by a business are considered to have a lifespan of four or five years. This means, in effect, that a quarter or a fifth of the item is being used up every year. If the whole cost were included in the first year, profits would be reduced. This wouldn't really show how well the business was doing. Instead, the P&L shows the proportion that is 'used up' each year. This is called **depreciation** and is included in Expenses. As the money was spent in a previous year, none actually leaves the business in the following years. It is just a way of spreading the cost over the years.

Work it out

1 When Jo buys her tables and chairs, what will have happened to her assets?

2 Why are tables and chairs different from her stocks of food?

3 If the £1000 appeared in her profit and loss account for this year, what effect would it have on her profit?

4 How can she show in each year's profit and loss account that the chairs have contributed to the business?

CALCULATING DEPRECIATION

There are several ways of calculating depreciation. The following are the two most commonly used.

- **The straight line method of calculating depreciation** simply means taking the selling price of the fixed asset away from the buying price and dividing this by the number of years you expect to own it. For example Jo bought the coach for £34 000 and expects its value to fall to £19 000 in five years when she would sell it. It would depreciate by £15 000 in five years. She would cost depreciation at £3000 a year.

Her net book value for the coach would fall by £3000 a year (see balance sheet). A computer would, of course, be written off completely as you would be unlikely to sell it.

- **The reducing balance method of calculating depreciation** better reflects the true second-hand value of the fixed assets as these usually lose most value in the early years and proportionately less in later years. This method reduces the amount by a fixed percentage each year.

Calculating depreciation

At end of financial year	Straight line method of calculating depreciation	Reducing balance method of calculating depreciation at 11% per year
2001	£31 000	£30 260
2002	£28 000	£26 931
2003	£25 000	£23 969
2004	£22 000	£21 332
2005	£19 000	£18 986

IN THE BALANCE SHEET

In the balance sheet the fixed assets will fall each year by the amount of depreciation. The resulting balance is called the **net book value**. The original cost of Jo's assets was £45 000 but depreciation reduces the net book value to £41 000 at the end of the first year, 30 April 2001.

Extract from Jo's Diner's balance sheet

Use of funds **Fixed assets**	At cost	Depreciation	Net book value
Computer	2500	500	2000
Coach	34 000	3000	31 000
Equipment	8500	500	8000
	45 000	**4000**	**41 000**

WHAT CAUSES DEPRECIATION?

- Wear and tear.
- Passing of time.
- Obsolescence.
- Lack of maintenance.

Work it out

1 Which of Jo's assets might suffer each form of depreciation?

2 Once an item has been written off, how does the business gain if the lifespan proves to be longer? What effect will this have on the profit?

3 Jo had aimed to write off her computer over five years but it became obsolete more quickly and she had to write it off in the third year. What effect would this have on her balance sheet and P&L?

Testing times: AQA

The following questions are adapted from AQA tests.

Assessment evidence	
C4	Create accurate final accounts from given data
E1	Identify why businesses need to keep accurate financial records
E5	Identify elements of working capital, cash flow and budgeting

Alan Perry, a sole trader, is a supplier of used cars. He has not kept accurate financial records and this has created a number of problems for those people who need to have information about the business.

Alan has recently appointed an accountant to help him maintain accurate financial records. He has asked his accountant to prepare a:

- trading and profit and loss account for the year ending 31 December 1999
- balance sheet on the 31 December 1999.

	Value £	Notes
Long term loan to business (repayable in 2006)	18 500	*Long term liability*
Rent and rates	9500	**Expense**
Stock held at 1 January 1999	75 000	**Expense**
Stock held at 31 December 1999	86 000	*Current asset*
Equipment (net book value at 31 December 1999)	208 000	*Fixed asset*
Fixtures & fittings (nbv at 31 December 1999)	264 000	*Fixed asset*
Staff costs	65 000	**Expense**
Interest payments	2000	**Expense**
Amount owing to suppliers	37 500	*Current liability*
Amount owing from customers	13 200	*Current asset*
Cash held by the business	3800	*Current asset*
Owner's capital (as at 1 January 1999)	339 000	*Source of finance*
Owner's drawings	28 000	
Turnover (sales revenue)	580 000	**Revenue**
Amount in bank accounts	7000	*Current asset*
Bank overdraft	500	*Current liability*
Purchases of goods during year	300 000	**Expense**

Italics = balance sheet

Bold = profit and loss. But also include stock held in P&L

CONSTRUCTING ACCOUNTS

1 Give two reasons why Alan should maintain accurate
financial records.   **2 marks**

Assessment evidence: E1

Help! A straightforward question asking for two facts.

Answer

Chose from the following:

> Accurate records will provide information from which Alan can see how
> financially healthy his business is.
>
> Potential investors would want a true picture of the business's
> performance, before they would part with their money.
>
> Alan would accurately be able to monitor what is happening and
> analyse the information to come up with improvements.
>
> Customers and suppliers may go to other businesses if the financial
> systems are not reliable.

Cheques and double checks
page 12 explains why
accuracy is important.

**Who's interested in the
accounts?** page 46 explains
why stakeholders are
interested in accounts.

2 The accountant has depreciated the fixed assets at 20% using the
reducing balance method. Calculate the net book value of each
of the two fixed assets by completing the shaded boxes.   **4 marks**

Assessment evidence: E5

Help! Depreciation is often thought to be about putting money on one side to replace
things. Don't be misled. It isn't! It is just a way of allocating the cost of equipment
in the years in which it contributes to output. The total cost is shown in the
balance sheet when the item is purchased, but it is shown in the profit and loss
account as an expense for each year it has been depreciated.

Wear and tear page 32
explains depreciation
methods.

Answer

nbv = net book value	nbv at 31 December 1999	Depreciation at 20%	nbv at 31 December 2000
Equipment	208 000	41 600	166 400
Fixtures & fittings	264 000	52 800	211 200

Help! Multiply each asset by **.2** to get 20%

3 Complete the following trading and profit and loss account and balance sheet. Information should be entered into the shaded boxes. **16 marks**

Assessment evidence: C4

What's the profit? page 30 explains how to build a profit and loss account.

 The profit and loss is the sum of activity in a business over a period of time. This tells us all about Alan Perry's cars over a year. It is quite simple. It just tells us how much money has come in, what it has been spent on and how much is left at the end of the year. You should use the amount set aside from depreciation from your answer to question 2.

The balance sheet is a snapshot at a moment in time. It shows where the finance has come from and how it is being used.

The working out is in the left-hand column and the totals are in the right-hand column. Remember that brackets mean you must subtract – or shows a loss.

Answer

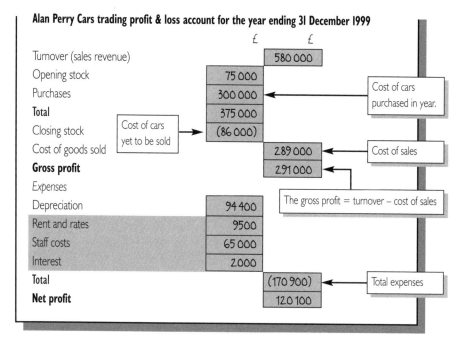

Alan Perry Cars trading profit & loss account for the year ending 31 December 1999

	£	£	
Turnover (sales revenue)		580 000	
Opening stock	75 000		
Purchases	300 000		Cost of cars purchased in year.
Total	375 000		
Closing stock	(86 000)		Cost of cars yet to be sold
Cost of goods sold		289 000	Cost of sales
Gross profit		291 000	
Expenses			
Depreciation	94 400		The gross profit = turnover – cost of sales
Rent and rates	9500		
Staff costs	65 000		
Interest	2000		
Total		(170 900)	Total expenses
Net profit		120 100	

Alan Perry Cars balance sheet as at 31 December 1999

	£	£
Fixed assets		
Equipment at net book value	166 400	
Fixtures and fittings at nbv	211 200	
Total		377 600

This is the value of the fixed assets after depreciation.

Current assets		
Stock	86 000	
Debtors	13 200	
Bank balance	7000	
Cash	3800	
Total		110 000

Total value of current assets.

Current liabilities		
Creditors	37 500	
Overdraft	500	
Total		(38 000)
Working capital (net current assets)		72 000
Long term liabilities		
Long term loan	(18 500)	
Net assets		431 100

In this case the net assets are calculated after taking off the long term loan, but some accounts work out the net assets without taking away the long term loan.

Financed by		
Capital	339 000	
Net profit	120 100	
Total		459 100
Less drawings	(28 000)	
Net worth		431 100

Alan has taken £28 000 for himself as a reward for his enterprise.

Testing times: Edexcel

The following questions are adapted from Edexcel tests.

Assessment evidence	
E5	Identify elements of working capital, cash flow and budgeting
E2	Identify different stakeholders and explain their interests in gaining financial information about the business
C4	Create accurate final accounts from given data

Is the balance right? page 26 explains how to build a balance sheet.

What's the profit? page 30 explains how to build a profit and loss account.

1 **Complete the following trading and profit and loss account and balance sheet prepared on 31 December 2000 for Peeko, a sole trader. Information should be entered into the shaded boxes.**

11 marks

Assessment Evidence: C4

Help! The profit and loss is the sum of activity in a business over a period of time. This tells us all about Peeko's activities over a year. It is quite simple. It just tells us how much money has come in, what it has been spent on and how much is left at the end of the year.

The balance sheet is a snapshot at a moment in time. It shows where the money has come from and how it is being used.

You need to use this reasoning to select from the information in the list below.

The working out is in the left-hand column and the totals are in the right-hand column. Remember that brackets mean you must subtract – or shows a loss.

Peeko sole trader	Value £	This space is for your workings	
Stock held at 1 January 2000	384		
Stock held at 31 December 2000	400		
Equipment (original cost)	8160		
Equipment (net book value at 31 December 2000)	6528		
Fixtures & fittings (original cost)	15120		
Fixtures & fittings (nbv at 31 December 2000)	12096		
Staff costs	2400		
Depreciation for the year	2976		
Amount owing to trade suppliers	3396		
Amount owing from trade customers	2880		
Cash held by the business	96		
Owner's capital (stake) (as at 1 January 2000)	16800		
Owner's drawings	11796		
Total invoices sent to trade customers	26400		
Amount in bank account	48		
Telephone bills	192		
Total invoices received from trade suppliers	7200		

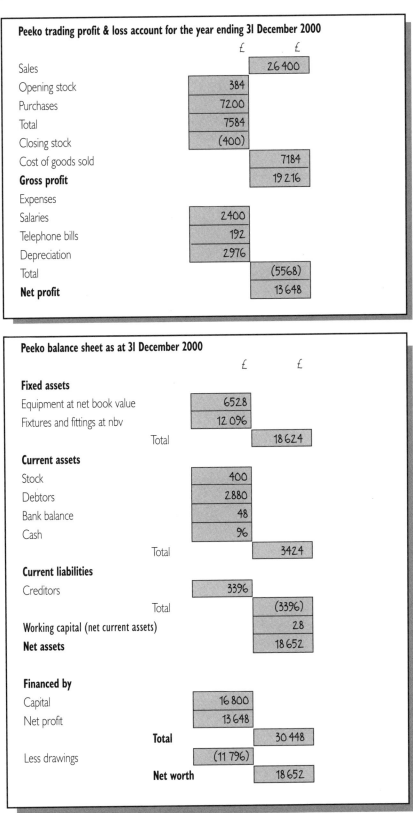

Peeko trading profit & loss account for the year ending 31 December 2000

	£	£
Sales		26 400
Opening stock	384	
Purchases	7200	
Total	7584	
Closing stock	(400)	
Cost of goods sold		7184
Gross profit		19 216
Expenses		
Salaries	2400	
Telephone bills	192	
Depreciation	2976	
Total		(5568)
Net profit		13 648

Peeko balance sheet as at 31 December 2000

	£	£
Fixed assets		
Equipment at net book value	6528	
Fixtures and fittings at nbv	12 096	
Total		18 624
Current assets		
Stock	400	
Debtors	2880	
Bank balance	48	
Cash	96	
Total		3424
Current liabilities		
Creditors	3396	
Total		(3396)
Working capital (net current assets)		28
Net assets		18 652
Financed by		
Capital	16 800	
Net profit	13 648	
Total		30 448
Less drawings	(11 796)	
Net worth		18 652

Wear and tear page 32 explains
depreciation methods.

2 Peeko depreciate their fixtures and fittings by 10% a year using
the straight line method of depreciation.
How much is charged for per year?   1 mark

Assessment evidence: E5

> **Help!** Depreciation is often thought to be about putting money on one side to replace
> things. Don't be misled. It isn't! It is just a way of allocating the cost of equipment
> in the years in which it contributes to output. It is in the balance sheet in total,
> but in the profit and loss account for the number of years over which it is being
> depreciated.

Answer

Each year Peeko depreciates its fixtures and fittings by 10% of the
original cost. It's the same amount each year because the business
uses the straight line method. The original cost of the fixtures and
fittings was £15 120 so depreciation is £1512 per year.

3 Why is the depreciation for Peeko recorded as an expense?   1 mark

Assessment evidence: E5

> **Help!** See note relating to question 2.

Answer

Depreciation is recorded as an expense in the profit and loss account
because it represents the proportion of the cost of equipment that has
been allocated to that year's production.

4 Briefly describe why Peeko's creditors and the Inland
Revenue have an interest in looking at Peeko's
financial information?   4 marks

Assessment evidence: E2

Cheques and double checks
page 12 explains the effect of
poor financial information on
creditors.

Who's interested in the accounts?
page 46 explains why
stakeholders are interested in
accounts.

> **Help!** This question is asking for reasons why two specific stakeholders are interested
> in the accounts. It isn't asking about VAT payments and refunds because these
> are administered by the Customs and Excise Department.

Answer

Peeko's creditors are the businesses it still owes money to. This will
include suppliers. They will want assurance that Peeko can pay its
bills on time and may wish to see Peeko's financial accounts before
doing business. The Inland Revenue has the job of collecting
corporation tax and will want to ensure that Peeko's accounts are
accurate and that it is paying the right amount of tax from its
profits.

Testing times: OCR

The following questions are adapted from OCR tests.

Assessment evidence	
E5	Identify elements of working capital, cash flow and budgeting
C7	Explain how businesses manage their working capital
C4	Create accurate final accounts from given data

Extract from the recommendations made to CD Productions Ltd to improve its financial management.

- Introduce a stock control system with a view to adopting Just In Time (JIT) wherever feasible.

- Set limits on credit terms for customers and negotiate favourable terms with suppliers.

---

1 **Name the elements that make up working capital.** **5 marks**

Assessment evidence: E5

Help! Straightforward question testing knowledge. Think of working capital as the resources that are imminently available for the business to use.

Answer

The working capital is made up of the current assets minus the current liabilities. The current assets include cash, stocks and debtors (usually customers who owe us money). The current liabilities include creditors (we owe money to) and an arranged bank overdraft.

Is the balance right? page 26 explains the elements that make up working capital.

---

2 **Explain the two suggestions made that would help CD Productions Ltd to manage their working capital more effectively.** **6 marks**

Assessment evidence: E5, C7

Help! You need to look at the component parts of working capital and explain how each can be managed more effectively. This involves speeding up the working capital cycle.

Answer

Introducing a new stock control system such as JIT will mean that stocks need only be ordered when the business needs them. There will be less money tied up in stocks because stock levels will be lower. This means we can operate with a lower working capital.

By setting limits on credit terms for customers, payments will be made sooner, making cash available for other uses. Negotiating more favourable terms with suppliers means either being able to delay payments by getting longer credit or it could mean us paying less for prompt payments. Each of these activities will speed up the working capital cycle.

Keeping the cash going page 82 explains what working capital is and how it should be managed.

Keeping the wolf from the door page 84 explains the working capital cycle.

3   Use the provided trial balance figures to complete the final
accounts for Fresh Ideas Ltd for 31 December 2000.
Enter your answers in the shaded boxes   8 marks

Assessment evidence: C4

 The trial balance brings together all the financial information from the business. It
then has to be allocated to the balance sheet and profit and loss account.
The profit and loss is the sum of activity in a business over a period of time. This
tells us all about Fresh Ideas Ltd's activities over a year. It is quite simple. It just
tells us how much money has come in, what it has been spent on and how
much is left at the end of the year.
The balance sheet is a snapshot at a moment in time. It shows where the
money has come from and how it is being used.
You need to use this reasoning to select from the information in the list below.
The working out is in the left-hand column and the totals are in the right-hand
column. Remember that brackets mean you must subtract – or shows a loss.

Answer

Abridged trial balance account	Dr (Debit)	Cr (Credit)
Sales		110 000
Purchases	55 050	
Stock held at 1 January 2000	12 000	
Expenses	43 000	
Buildings (net book value)	50 000	
Plant and machinery (nbv)	80 000	
Vehicles (nbv)	30 000	
Debtors	25 000	
Creditors		30 000
Bank	1200	
Cash	250	
Capital at 1 January 2000		160 000
Retained profits at 1 January 2000		6500
Drawings	10 000	
Total	306 500	306 500

Stock at 31 December 2000 was valued at £15 000

**From ledgers to final
accounts** page 24 explains
how the trial balance is
drawn up.

Is the balance right? page 26
explains how to build a
balance sheet.

What's the profit? page 30
explains how to build a
profit and loss account.

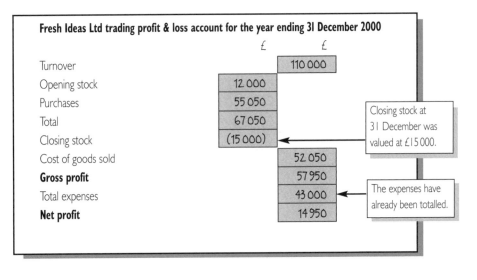

Fresh Ideas Ltd trading profit & loss account for the year ending 31 December 2000

	£	£
Turnover		110 000
Opening stock	12 000	
Purchases	55 050	
Total	67 050	
Closing stock	(15 000)	
Cost of goods sold		52 050
Gross profit		57 950
Total expenses		43 000
Net profit		14 950

Closing stock at 31 December was valued at £15 000.

The expenses have already been totalled.

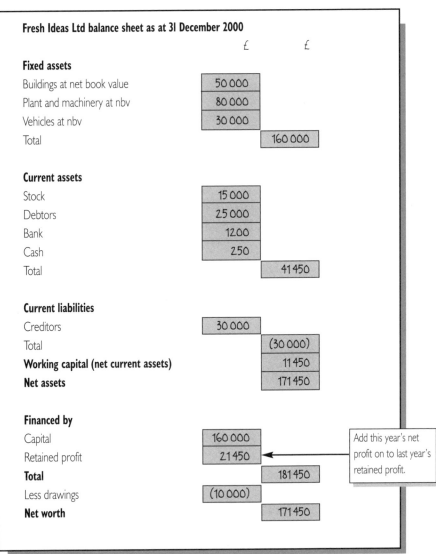

Fresh Ideas Ltd balance sheet as at 31 December 2000

	£	£
Fixed assets		
Buildings at net book value	50 000	
Plant and machinery at nbv	80 000	
Vehicles at nbv	30 000	
Total		160 000
Current assets		
Stock	15 000	
Debtors	25 000	
Bank	1200	
Cash	250	
Total		41 450
Current liabilities		
Creditors	30 000	
Total		(30 000)
Working capital (net current assets)		11 450
Net assets		171 450
Financed by		
Capital	160 000	
Retained profit	21 450	
Total		181 450
Less drawings	(10 000)	
Net worth		171 450

Add this year's net profit on to last year's retained profit.

Testing times: practice questions

Better Badges was a mini-enterprise company selling badges to the pupils within their school. Sarah was good at art and she could draw some fetching cartoons. Jack had a way with words and, with Sarah, made some hilarious badge designs. Lots of children said they would buy a badge.

The business started on 1 April. After trading for four weeks they wanted to know how well they were doing. Fortunately, Jade, the finance manager, kept a record of money transactions, but it was just scribbled into her note book. She needs some help in sorting it all out.

A badge-making machine – second hand for only £20.
All team members to buy a share, making £12 worth of shares.
Bank loan £13.
Interest on loan £0.50 pence.
Wages £34.50.
£1 for photocopying posters.
Rent of room H12 was £4.
Turnover from selling badges £75.
IOU from Geography teachers £2.50 (pay up or else!).
Cost of all the stock bought = £35.
We owe supplier £7.50.
Bank balance £8.

Jade opened the cash box and counted out £2.00.

Complete the following tasks in pencil.

1 Use the above information to help construct the trial balance below. Fill in shaded boxes only. Assume the owners have made no drawings and there is no depreciation.

Trial balance at 28 April	Debit	Credit
Sales		
Purchases		
Bank balance at 28 April		
Expenses (interest, wages, rent, posters)		
Fixed assets (badge-making machine)		
Debtors (money owed by customers)		
Creditors (money owed to suppliers)		
Cash		
Bank loan		
Owners' capital at 28 April		
Total		

2 Use the information in the trial balance to help construct the balance sheet and profit and loss accounts.

Some hints.

Complete the profit and loss first in order to calculate the net profit.

Since no drawings are made, the net profit becomes retained profit and this value is entered in the balance sheet.

3 Alter the final accounts to reflect the following:

the Geography teachers pay up

Better Badges sends a remittance advice along with a cheque of £7.50 to the suppliers to settle the invoice.

4 What has happened to the net profit?

5 What has happened to the balance sheet?

6 The owners decide to make drawings of £6.50. Make the changes to the final accounts.

7 What has now happened to the net worth and net assets of Better Badges?

8 If the badge-making machine had depreciated by £1 how would this alter both final accounts?

Who's interested in the accounts?

What's it all about?

You need to understand why stakeholders, including both internal and external users, need financial information.

'Have we any overdue payments?'

'Have we received a credit note for those faulty supplies? Good, but I'll check up with the warehouse to see if the new delivery has arrived.'

'Who owes us money? OK, I'll get onto them straight away.'

Work it out

1. How can the business check on overdue payments?
2. Who might want to know this information?
3. How might you approach a customer who owes you money?

'So you want to increase the overdraft to buy materials for the new order. It will take you a month to make and you won't get paid until 28 days after delivery. I'd like to see your cash flow forecast and...'

Work it out

1. What other documents might the business need to show the bank manager?
2. Why would the bank manager want to make a careful check on the business?

WHO WANTS TO KNOW?

Financial information has to be honest and accurate. It can serve several purposes for different groups of people. Some may wish to check that the business finances are properly done and have met legal requirements. This means that the accounts are fair and people won't be cheated. Others may wish to check on how well the business is performing by looking for patterns or trends in the accounts. All these groups of people have an interest or stake in the success of the business so they are called **stakeholders**.

Stakeholder interest in accounts

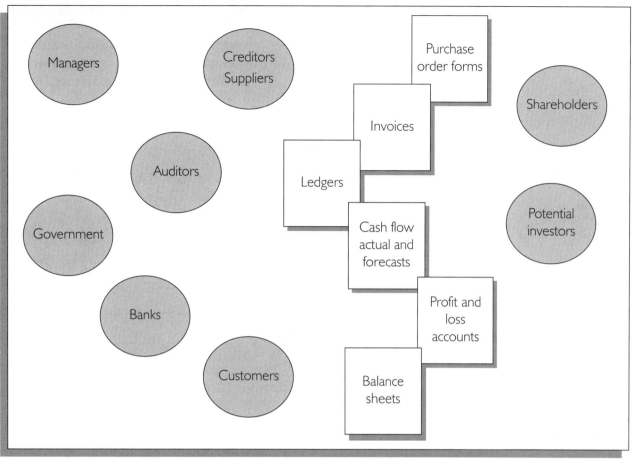

The managers are **internal users** of the information. Managers will want to make sure bills are paid on time to keep suppliers happy. They will want to make sure that enough money is coming in to pay the bills. They will want to know about the health of the business so they can set targets to improve the performance of the business.

People outside the business that need to know about the financial information are called **external users**.

- Creditors are the businesses that are owed money for goods and services supplied on credit. Suppliers may look at whether the business pays its bills on time.

- Auditors check that the record keeping is accurate and honest.

- Government calculates that it receives the correct tax.

- Banks, who provide loans and overdrafts, need to know if they will get their money back.

- Customers will not want the business they buy from to stop trading.

- Shareholders will want to know what type of return they will be getting.

- Potential investors will want to compare businesses before putting their money into one.

Both managers and external users are mainly interested in looking at sets of financial information rather than individual financial documents, because these can be used to monitor the performance of the business (how well it is doing) over a time period or in comparison with other businesses. These sets of information are called **final accounts**. Remember that they are constructed from all the original documents. We will explore how to measure performance in the next few pages.

Public Limited Companies must publish their financial accounts and you can access these from their websites. The *bized* website at *www.bized.ac.uk* is a good source of information on large companies. However, annual reports and financial data are written in a language, detail and style for certain stakeholders such as shareholders and investors. They may be confusing. Look for the main headings.

How profitable is it?

Business X

Well we made £10 000, that's brilliant.

Business Y

Only £10 000, that's pathetic.

Work it out

1. How can both comments be right?
2. What other information would you need to give you a clear picture of the profitability of each business?

IS IT REALLY PROFITABLE?

Profit is needed for the long term survival of a business. Profit provides a reward for the investors and is also a source of funds to help the business expand. The managers of a business will want to know how profitable it is, so will other stakeholders like the bank, shareholders and potential customers. A few small calculations will tell a business just where it stands.

PROFITABILITY RATIOS

To make a more valid comparison we need to look at the figures more closely. In the chart in the next column the relationship between the figures is converted to percentages. The percentages are known as **ratios**.

The profit here is net profit. It has been calculated by taking away all the costs before tax is paid.

The **net profit margin** $= \dfrac{\text{net profit}}{\text{turnover (sales)}} \times 100$

This will give you a percentage.

An **operating profit margin** can also be worked out by replacing net profit with operating profit.

The **net profit margin** measures the business's net profit as a percentage of sales or turnover. It tells the business how much the business earns for every £1 of sales after paying the cost of the sales and the expenses. If the business can reduce its expenses the net profit margin will improve.

Net profit margins compared

Business X

| Turnover £100 000 (100%) | Costs £90 000 (90%) |
| | profit £10 000 (10%) |

How many times will the profit fit into the turnover?

Business Y

| Turnover £200 000 (100%) | Costs £190 000 (95%) |
| | profit £10 000 (5%) |

Work it out

1. If in a year's time business Y had increased its net profit to £15 000 and increased its turnover to £120 000 calculate its new net profit margin.
2. Has this gone up or down?
3. Is this a good or bad thing?

The **gross profit margin** measures the business's gross profit as a percentage of sales or turnover. The gross profit margin will improve if the business can buy cheaper supplies or if it can raise prices.

$$\text{gross profit margin} = \frac{\text{gross profit}}{\text{sales revenue or turnover}} \times 100$$

For Jo's Diner for the financial year ending April 2001 this is

$$\frac{58\,000}{110\,000} \times 100 = 52.7\%$$

For Jo's Diner for the financial year ending April 2002 this is

$$\frac{56\,000}{130\,000} \times 100 = 43\%$$

The lower ratio in 2002 means the cost of supplies has risen by a greater percentage than sales.

Jo's Diner profit and loss account year ending 30 April 2001

Turnover (sales revenue)			110 000
Cost of sales			
	Opening stock	0	
	Purchases	62 000	
	Closing stock	(10 000)	
			52 000
Gross profit			**58 000**
Expenses			
	Insurance	6000	
	Depreciation	4000	
(Includes net interest payments) Other expenses		35 000	
			(45 000)
Net profit			**13 000**

For 2001

Turnover £110 000	Cost of sales £52 000	Cost of sales £52 000
	Gross profit £58 000	Expenses £45 000
		Net profit £13 000

ONE YEAR LATER

Jo's Diner profit and loss account year ending 30 April 2002

Turnover (sales revenue)			130 000
Cost of sales			
	Opening stock	10 000	
	Purchases	67 000	
	Sub total	77 000	
	Closing stock	(3000)	
			74 000
Gross profit			**56 000**
Expenses			
	Insurance	6000	
	Depreciation	4000	
(Includes net interest payments) Other expenses		38 000	
			(48 000)
Net profit			**8000**

One year later (2002)

Turnover £130 000	Cost of sales £74 000	Cost of sales £74 000
	Gross profit £56 000	Expenses £48 000
		Net profit £8000

DO BUSINESSES NEED THE SAME LEVEL OF PROFIT?

Some businesses need more profits because they need funds for research and development. Pharmaceutical industries, for example, have long testing periods for their drugs. Telecommunications companies need to invest heavily in capital assets. This makes it important to compare businesses in competition with each other, for example Tesco, Sainsbury and Safeway.

Work it out

1 What do you notice about the proportion of net profit to turnover for the two figures above?

2 Calculate the net profit margin in 2001.

2 Jo has increased turnover by 18% but her costs have risen by 20.5% – enough to lower her profits significantly. Which increases in costs did the most damage? Her expenses have increased by just over 6% but cost of sales by nearly 30%. Calculate Jo's new net profit margin for 2002.

4 What has contributed to the decline in profits?

5 Can Jo do anything about it?

Is it solvent?

What's it all about?

You need to know how to calculate a current ratio in order to understand the solvency of a business.

'Sorry, we can't extend your loan.'

ORDERS
ORDERS
UNPAID INVOICES
UNPAID BILLS
MANAGER

Work it out

1 What or who are creditors?

2 Why might the bank not wish to extend the loan?

3 What might the business have done to make sure this did not happen?

SURVIVING

While profit is necessary for the long term survival of a business, day to day survival depends on finding enough finance to pay all the outstanding debts or liabilities when they are due. If it can do this, it is **solvent**. A business must keep its solvency under regular review. A failure to pay **creditors** can lead to **liquidation** or **bankruptcy**, even with healthy orders and good profits.

- **Bankruptcy** happens to sole traders or partnerships when they are unable to pay their debts to creditors. The owner of the business may have to sell the house and other personal assets to pay the bills. Something to be avoided!

- **Liquidation** is the term used when a limited company fails. All the assets are sold off and the proceeds are paid to the creditors. The creditors may not get back all the money they are owed. The owners of the

business do not lose all their possessions because their responsibility is 'limited' to the money (capital) they have put into the business.

SIGNS OF INSOLVENCY

Customers, suppliers, employees and the bank all have a stake in the solvency of a business. There are some clues that suggest a business is in trouble:

- Late in paying wages;
- Overdue in paying invoices;
- Asking suppliers for far more than 30 days' credit;
- Stocks build up;
- Continually trying to borrow more from the bank.

A supplier might pay a specialist company to run a credit check on a potential customer to find out if it pays bills reliably.

Work it out

Draw up a spider diagram explaining why each stakeholder has an interest in the solvency of a business.

BUT ARE WE SOLVENT?

Managers use figures in the balance sheet to find out if the business is solvent. The easiest check is to take away the current liabilities from the current assets. What is left is the **working capital**. It must be positive.

Jo's balance sheet looks like this. How do her current assets and liabilities compare?

Current assets	
Stock	10 000
Debtors	9000
Bank	3000
Cash	1500
	23 500
Current liabilities	
Creditors	8500
Working Capital	**15 000**

MAKING A COMPARISON

A manager wants to compare solvency over time to see if it is changing. The relationship between current assets and current liabilities is known as the **current ratio**. It tells you how much you have in current assets for every £ of short term liabilities.

Current ratio

= current assets : current liabilities

23 500 : 8500 = 2.76 : 1

This means the business has £2.76 of current assets for every £1 it owes.

This is a very safe position to be in as accountants consider 1.5 : 1 to be fine.

This is a comparison at a particular time and the more often it can be done the better. Before buying her tables and chairs on a short term loan, the ratio was

23 500 : 5500
= 4.27 : 1

CAN THINGS BE BETTER?

Jo has working capital of £15 000 but she might look at the balance of her current assets. Does the business really need £10 000 worth of stock? Perhaps £3000 of stock is enough if deliveries can be made on time. If stocks were cut, you would free up £7000 in cash that could be used for something else.

Work it out

1 Complete the calculation.
  The next year, the current assets were valued at £12 000 and the current liabilities were valued at £10 000. The business has £.?. of assets for every £1 it owes.

2 Can the business cover its debts?

3 Why is this probably a better ratio than the previous year?

4 If the current ratio falls below 1.5 : 1, what should the business do?

Keeping close control

'But this won't help me pay the bills.'

What's it all about?

You need to be able to calculate an acid test ratio, stock turnover ratio and selling and debt collection periods in order to understand the solvency of a business.

Work it out

1 What items are included in current assets?

2 Which can be used to pay creditors immediately?

3 Which can be used to pay creditors in the longer term? What problems might arise in relying on these assets?

IS A CURRENT RATIO ENOUGH?

The current ratio seems a good method to check on solvency, but look back to the balance sheet on page 27. The stock was valued at £10 000. Stock is not always easy to shift. Perhaps turnover shows that sales are falling or are below expectations. Businesses selling cars and furniture, for example, find stock shifts slowly. Have a look at the box on stock turnover. For these types of business it is better to take away stock from the calculations. The ratio that does this is called the acid test ratio:

$$\text{acid test ratio} = \frac{\text{current assets} - \text{stock}}{\text{current liabilities}}$$

In our example = £23 500 − £10 000 : £8500

= 1.59 : 1

So the business has £1.59 for every £1 it owes. For businesses with a slow stock turnover the ratio needs to be above 1:1. A business with a fast rate of stock turnover would probably use the current ratio.

The rate of stock turnover tells you how quickly a business shifts it stock. It is worked out using the following formula: $\dfrac{\text{cost of sales}}{\text{average stock}}$

See page 82 to find out more about the rate of stock turnover.

Work it out

1 Which solvency ratio should each of the following types of business use?
- Supermarkets
- Car sales
- Aeroplane manufacturers
- Bakers
- Newspapers

2 Why might banks wish to see the balance sheets of businesses that ask for an overdraft facility?

3 A greengrocer may sell most of his stock everyday so his stock turnover might be 300 as he is closed some days. What about car sales?

CHASING THE DEBTS

Chasing debt is a problem for many businesses. A credit controller may be employed to pursue people who have not paid up.

An **aged debtor** is overdue in paying the money it owes your business. A debt that is long overdue may have to be written off as a **bad debt** because the debtor won't pay up. A bad debt cannot be counted as a current asset in the balance sheet. It must show up as an expense in the profit and loss account (see page 30).

The effectiveness of the credit controller can be judged by changes in the **debtors' collection period** or **debtor days**. This is a ratio that measures the average time debtors take to pay their outstanding balances. It should get shorter. A manager would use this information alongside the aged debtor information. Debtor days alone may hide the fact that you have a few very overdue payments.

$$\text{debtors' collection period} = \frac{\text{debtors}}{\text{sales}} \times 365 \text{ days}$$
(or debtor days)

Work it out

If credit sales for the year was £28 000 and the debtors at the end of the year were 3000 then

$$\frac{3000}{28\,000} \times 365 = 39 \text{ days}$$

If a year ago the figure was 32 days:

1 Has the ratio improved or worsened?

2 What could be done about it?

Work it out

1 If you were the credit controller for A&B Textiles, and Hatrick had just made an order for £2000 worth of textiles, what would you check on before the order was accepted?

2 What effect will poor **credit control** have on a business's working capital and its solvency?

3 Why does a credit controller have to be good with customers, accurate and able to meet deadlines?

Statement of account   **A&B Textiles**

To: Hatrick
Unit 5
Elmhurst Trading Estate
Southampton

123 Park Street, Bradford

Date: 30/5/01
Account number: Hat22
Reference: 56754

28 days to settle invoices

> Hatrick didn't settle its April bill in April. The sum is added on to what is due in May. A&B Textiles will want a full payment.

Date	Details	Debit	Credit	Balance
1/4/01	Previous balance			£308.78
3/4/01	Cheque received		£308.78	£0.00
9/4/01	Goods supplied invoice 6659	£405.78		£405.78
7/5/01	Credit note Y45		£74.00	£331.78
29/5/01	Goods supplied on invoice 6678	£216.87		£548.65

Hatrick's aged debtor analysis at 1/6/01

Owing up to 1 month	Owing 1–2 months
£142.87	£331.78

> Outstanding balance is the sum still owing.

What's the return?

Work it out

1 Which business do you think is doing better?
2 Why?

MAKING CAPITAL WORK

One way of looking at a business is to find out how hard its capital is working. The information to work this out comes from both the balance sheet and the profit and loss account.

Return on capital employed or ROCE for short tells you a bit about how the business is performing by looking at the amount of profit that has been made compared with the amount of capital being used. **Capital employed** includes share capital, reserves and long term loans.

This ratio is of special interest to shareholders, potential investors in the business and banks.

$$ROCE = \frac{Operating\ or\ net\ profit}{Capital\ employed} \times 100$$

Business		Year 2000
X	Capital employed	£480m
	Operating profit	£40m
	ROCE %	8.3%

Work it out

1 Complete the table in the next column for businesses Y and Z.
2 Which one has the highest ROCE?

WHY BOTHER WITH ROCE?

Profit figures are not enough on their own. A business with lots of capital should be making lots of profit. ROCE tells you whether it is using its capital efficiently.

People will want to invest in a business with a higher ROCE because it is making more profit from its capital. Keeping smaller stocks, for example, would mean that the business either:

■ needed less capital; or

■ could use the capital for something more productive.

An investor will compare the ROCE of various businesses before making a decision about where to invest. The decision will also take into account the degree of risk. A risky business might have a high ROCE but who knows what will happen next year?

Business		Year	2000
Y	Capital employed		£300m
	Operating profit		£15m
	ROCE %		
Z	Capital employed		£400m
	Operating profit		
	ROCE %		10%

Business	Year	2000	1999	Percentage change
Tesco	Capital employed	£6382m	£5624m	13.5%
	Operating profit	£1030m	£934m	10.3%
	ROCE %	16.1%	16.6%	−3.0%

Business	Year	2000	1999	Percentage change
Sainsbury	Capital employed	£4791m	£4689m	2.2%
	Operating profit	£640m	£857m	−25.3%
	ROCE %	13.4%	18.3%	−26.8%

Business	Year	2000	1999	Percentage change
Safeway	Capital employed	£3070m	£2946m	4.2%
	Operating profit	£317m	£423m	−25.1%
	ROCE %	10.3%	14.4%	−28.5%

Work it out

1 Which has the best ROCE in each year and which has the worst?

2 What are the trends of each business?

3 Do you think the supermarket business became more or less competitive in 2000?

WORKING ASSETS

Asset turnover is used to find out how well the fixed assets of the business are working. It measures the ratio of sales to fixed assets. If the asset turnover figure falls, the fixed assets are being used less effectively because they are not generating as many sales. A business might try to improve efficiency by operating shifts or by better training.

$$\text{Asset turnover} = \frac{\text{sales}}{\text{net assets}}$$

$$\text{For 1998} = \frac{£100\,000}{£20\,000} = 5$$

Work it out

Using the figures in the table below:

1 Complete the ratios for 1999 and 2000.

2 What happened to the ratios?

Year	1998	1999	2000
Sales	£100 000	£110 000	£112 000
Fixed assets	£20 000	£18 000	£22 000
Asset turnover	5		

In 1999 the fixed assets depreciated by £2000. More were bought in 2000.

A WORD OF WARNING

Consider the ROCE of a street juggler. It will be enormous, simply because the busker's total capital investment will only be the juggling equipment.

■ It is important to compare the size and nature of the business.

■ It is more realistic to compare a business with a similar one.

■ It is dangerous to just use one ratio. It is best to use a combination of ratios.

■ Ratios tell us what has happened in the past, not what is happening now.

HINTS TO UNDERSTANDING THE FIGURES

■ Has the ratio increased, decreased or stayed about the same?

■ What has been the percentage change?

What a performance!
Act 1

'Who would you put your money on?'

What's it all about?

You need to be able to understand and explain why investors hold shares in a public limited company and how their dividends are determined.

WHO OR WHAT ARE INVESTORS?

If a company wants to expand, it can raise money or capital by issuing new shares to investors. Individuals and organisations can buy shares in a business. When they do so, they become **shareholders**. In return for holding shares the investor will expect some reward. The reward is known as a **dividend**. It is paid every six months or on a yearly basis for each share owned. The investor will also hope that the value of the shares will rise so they can be sold for more than the investor paid.

Investors include:

- individuals;
- employees' pension funds;
- insurance businesses;
- other businesses.

HOW DO INDIVIDUALS MAKE INVESTMENTS IN COMPANIES?

- Buy shares of any plc.

Work it out

1 Make a list of all the factors that would persuade you to buy shares in one company rather than another.

2 Where would you look to find out the answers to your questions?

3 From the information you have already, which business would you put your money into? Why?

- Buy equity ISAs. You put your money into the hands of a financial provider who buys shares in a range of companies. If the shares go up, so does the value of your ISA.

- If you have life insurance or a pension, the money will be used to buy and sell shares, so the value of your policy increases.

About one third of Tesco's shareholders are its employees but they own less than 3% of the shares. Other individuals represent just over half the shareholders and they own less than 8% of the shares. This leaves 89% of Tesco shares in the hands of institutions such as banks, insurance companies and pension funds.

CAN YOU BUY INTO ANY BUSINESS?

No! Some businesses are **private limited companies**. Their shareholders can decide who can buy the shares. You can buy shares in a **public limited company**, a plc.

If you buy shares through the **Stock Exchange**, you are buying existing shares owned by an investor who wants to sell. In this case you are not buying from the business itself so it is not raising capital for the business. The Stock Exchange is a second-hand market for shares. It is, however, important because the share price of a business tells us about its value.

If a business wishes to raise capital it can arrange to issue new shares. Investors will only buy the new shares if they think the business will do well.

WHERE CAN YOU FIND OUT INFORMATION ABOUT A PLC?

All plcs have to issue Annual Reports which are available to everyone. They are often on their website.

J Sainsbury plc website, like many others, makes financial information available to investors.

WHAT IS A DIVIDEND AND HOW IS IT DETERMINED?

The dividend is paid to each shareholder at the end of an accounting period. It is expressed as the number of pence per share. The dividend is paid from a company's profit after tax. For example J Sainsbury plc made a post-tax profit of £598m in 1999. Some £304m was retained by the company leaving the remaining £294m to go to the shareholders. Each share was allocated 14.32p as a dividend. You would think that the greater the profit the more the dividend paid, but it is not that simple. In 2000 J Sainsbury's profits after tax were much lower at £347m, but they gave out a similar dividend because keeping the shareholders happy was important.

Work it out

J Sainsbury plc's dividends

Financial Year	94/5	95/6	96/7	97/8	98/9	99/00
Dividend	11.70p	12.10p	12.30p	13.90p	14.32p	14.32p

1 What has happened to the value of the dividend over the years?

2 Why might the dividend have not increased in 2000?

3 Why would you also want to know the price of a share when looking at dividends?

What a performance!
Act 2

'Who would you put your money on?'

What's it all about?

You need to know what investors and shareholders in a plc look for when assessing the overall performance of a business, such as share prices and price earnings ratios.

Work it out

1 Have a look at Tesco's and Sainsbury's websites and find out how they are doing.

2 What other factors can you find there to provide you with information that might persuade you to buy the shares?

WHY ISSUE SHARES?

A company will issue shares to raise capital for investments. The shares are sold to investors at a set price. The money raised will be used for investment projects such as building a new factory, research and development, or buying new machinery.

The shareholder can sell the shares to other investors through the Stock Exchange. The price will be determined by the market. If there are more sellers than buyers the share price will fall. If there are more buyers than sellers the share price will rise.

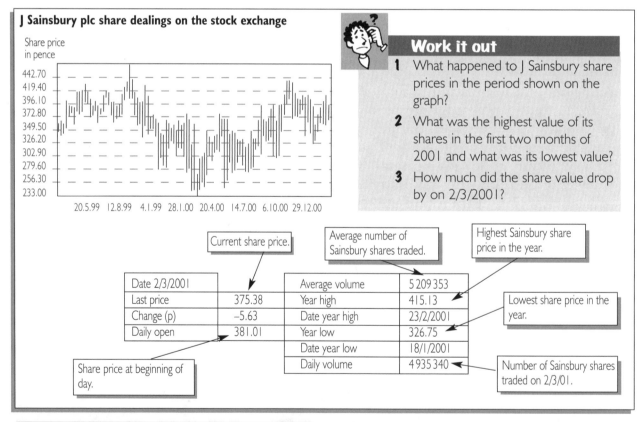

J Sainsbury plc share dealings on the stock exchange

Share price in pence

442.70
419.40
396.10
372.80
349.50
326.20
302.90
279.60
256.30
233.00

20.5.99 12.8.99 4.1.99 28.1.00 20.4.00 14.7.00 6.10.00 29.12.00

Work it out

1 What happened to J Sainsbury share prices in the period shown on the graph?

2 What was the highest value of its shares in the first two months of 2001 and what was its lowest value?

3 How much did the share value drop by on 2/3/2001?

Current share price.

Average number of Sainsbury shares traded.

Highest Sainsbury share price in the year.

Date 2/3/2001		Average volume	5 209 353
Last price	375.38	Year high	415.13
Change (p)	−5.63	Date year high	23/2/2001
Daily open	381.01	Year low	326.75
		Date year low	18/1/2001
		Daily volume	4 935 340

Lowest share price in the year.

Share price at beginning of day.

Number of Sainsbury shares traded on 2/3/01.

WHAT DETERMINES SHARE PRICE?

There are four main ingredients that determine the value of J Sainsbury plc share prices.

■ The general performance of the Stock Market.

■ The general performance of supermarkets.

■ The performance of J Sainsbury plc compared with the other supermarkets.

■ How investors believe J Sainsbury plc will perform in the future.

Data can be found in the financial section of the annual reports. But take care – accounts are often displayed in different ways.

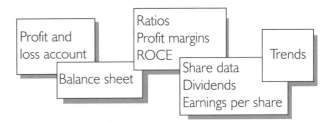

Financial information for three supermarkets

Company	Year	2000	1999	Percentage change
Tesco	Sales turnover	£18796m	£17158	9.5%
	Operating profit	£1030m	£934m	10.3%
	Operating profit margin	5.5%	5.4%	1.9%
Sainsbury	Sales turnover	£16271m	£16433m	–1%
	Operating profit	£640m	£857m	–25.3%
	Operating profit margin	3.9%	5.2%	–25%
Safeway	Sales turnover	£7659m	£7510m	2%
	Operating profit	£317m	£423	–25.1%
	Operating profit margin	4.1%	5.6%	–26.8%

Company	Year	2000	1999	Percentage change
Tesco	Dividend per share	4.48p	4.12p	8.7%
	Earnings per share	10.18p	9.37p	8.6%
Sainsbury	Dividend per share	13.2p	13.2p	0%
	Earnings per share	18.3p	29.2p	–37.3%
Safeway	Dividend per share	8.64p	14.4%	–40%
	Earnings per share	17.1p	23.8p	–28.2%

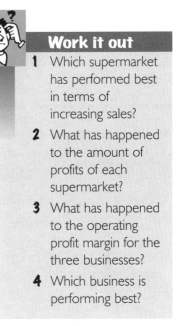

Work it out

1 Which supermarket has performed best in terms of increasing sales?

2 What has happened to the amount of profits of each supermarket?

3 What has happened to the operating profit margin for the three businesses?

4 Which business is performing best?

The dividend per share looks quite low for Tesco, but its profit margin and ROCE were the best. Are their shareholders being given a bad deal? It's hard to answer – because you need some more information.

■ **Earnings per share** compares the post-tax profit with the number of shares in the business so you can see how much each share 'earns'. Tesco has increased its earnings per share whilst the other two supermarkets have seen a large drop in theirs.

■ **Price earnings ratio** measures the current market price divided by the earnings per share. As share prices rise when investors are confident, a high p/e ratio suggests that people think the future for the company is bright.

You would also need to look at how the share price is changing because this might suggest what other investors believe will happen. As one of the factors which determines share price is the performance of the business, potential investors will want to know if the company is meeting its objectives.

Have a look at Tesco's website to find out how it is doing. www.tesco.co.uk. Do you think Tesco is meeting its objectives?

Share information

7 March 2001	Share price	Earnings per share	Price earnings ratio
Tesco	259	10.79	24.0
Sainsbury	370	17.50	21.1
Safeway	286	18.45	15.5

Work it out

1 What determines the price of a share?

2 What factors persuade potential shareholders to buy a particular share?

3 Which stakeholders are interested in share prices and price earnings ratios? Why?

4 Why should a company be concerned about the value of its shares?

Testing times: AQA

The following are adapted from AQA tests.

Assessment evidence	
E4	Identify appropriate financial information and use it to calculate performance, solvency and profitability ratios
C5	Explain how financial ratios are used by different groups of stakeholders to interpret financial data
C6	Compare and evaluate ratios in different businesses over time
A3	Explain why ratios change over time and how this affects different groups of stakeholders
A4	Draw conclusions about the financial performance of the business based on your use and understanding of a range of financial data

Extracted from the Pizza Express Chief Executive's Report

During the year to June 1999 over 1000 new staff joined the company as 40 new restaurants were opened in the UK and in Pakistan, Russia, Switzerland, Turkey and the USA.

This growth saw an improvement in our net profit compared with the previous year.

In 1999 the company served 13 million customers and expects to welcome more in the coming year as we have plans to open a further 55 restaurants.

Pizza Express profit and loss account	1999 £m	1998 £m
Turnover	126.60	99.60
Cost of sales	90.00	70.70
Gross profit	**36.60**	**28.90**
Distribution costs	2.80	2.30
Administration expenses	4.70	4.50
Net profit before interest and taxation	**29.10**	**22.10**
Interest payable	0.30	0.30
Corporation tax	5.90	4.80
Net profit after interest and taxation	**22.90**	**17.00**
Dividends paid	3.70	2.80
Retained profit	19.20	14.20

Earnings per share 1999
33.7p

Earnings per share 1998
26.7p

Pizza Express balance sheet as at 30 June	1999 £m	1998 £m
Fixed assets		
Tangible assets	84.7	65.4
Investments in other businesses	–0.1	0.3
	84.6	65.7
Current assets		
Stocks	5.1	4.1
Debtors	4.7	5.0
Cash in bank and in hand	6.2	5.4
	16.0	14.5
Current liabilities		
Creditors	33.5	39.9
Net assets employed	**67.1**	**40.3**
Financed by		
Long term liabilities	0.1	3.5
Shareholders' funds	67.0	36.8
Capital employed	**67.1**	**40.3**

Source: Pizza Express plc annual report and accounts 1999

1 Calculate Pizza Express' working capital for 1998 and 1999.

2 marks

Assessment evidence: E4

Help! Straightforward question testing knowledge. Think of working capital as the resources that are imminently available for the business to use.

Answer

Working capital is the difference between the current assets and the current liabilities. In 1998 this was a negative figure (£25.4m) and this deficit was reduced to (£17.5m) in 1999.

Is the balance right? page 26 explains the elements that make up working capital.

2 Explain two ways in which Pizza Express might improve its position with regard to working capital.

6 marks

Assessment evidence: C7

Help! You need to look at the component parts of working capital and explain how each can be managed more effectively. This involves speeding up the working capital cycle. You could develop your answer to include creditor days and debtor days (see page 83).

Answer

Pizza Express seems to have a poor working capital position. It would be unable to find cash in the short term if all its creditors demanded payment. It is not clear whether the creditors in the extract from the accounts includes overdrafts with banks. If not, Pizza Express could seek to arrange overdrafts.

Another solution would be to speed up the working capital cycle using one of the following methods.

Introducing a new stock control system such as JIT will mean that stocks need only be ordered when the business needs them. There will be less money tied up in stocks because stock levels will be lower. This means they can operate with a lower working capital. However, stock levels do not seem that high.

By setting limits on credit terms for customers, payments will be made sooner, making cash available for other uses. However, debtor days are quite low.

Negotiating more favourable terms with suppliers means either being able to delay payments by getting longer credit, or it could mean paying less for prompt payments. Each of these activities will speed up the working capital cycle. However, Pizza Express already has a high creditor days ratio.

Maybe this type of industry operates on quite a low liquidity. Pizza Express will compare its levels with similar companies operating in the same industry.

Keeping the cash going page 82 explains what working capital is and how it should be managed. Page 83 explains debtor and creditor days.

Keeping the wolf from the door page 84 explains the working capital cycle.

3 Calculate the following ratios for Pizza Express for 1998 and 1999 (display your answers to two decimal places). **6 marks**

Assessment evidence: E4

1 ROCE = (net profit before interest and taxation/capital employed) x 100.
2 Net profit margin = (net profit before interest and taxation/turnover) x 100.
3 Asset turnover = (turnover/net assets employed).

 Simple calculations drawing on the information in the data provided.

Answer

	1999	1998
ROCE	43.37%	54.84%
Net profit margin	22.99%	22.19%
Asset turnover	1.89 times	2.47 times

4 A number of different stakeholders will analyse the ratios you have calculated along with other parts of Pizza Express' financial report. Explain two possible reasons why the ROCE has changed. **6 marks**

Assessment evidence: C6

Help! You are being asked to analyse the information provided by the ratio. Look at the two elements which make up the ratio and see what might have changed.

Answer

Massive expansion programme as shown by fixed assets rising by nearly £20m. It takes time for the new business outlets to establish new customers. Pizza Express has also expanded into unsure market areas, e.g. Pakistan, and this may be even slower to build up a customer base. The company has invested capital into opening 40 new outlets at various times throughout the year so most haven't had a year's trading figures. These outlets will be expected to make an impact next year. It could be a very competitive market, squeezing profits, but this is not reflected in the slight increase in the net profit margin.

How profitable is it? page 48 explains profit margins.

What's the return? pages 54–55 explains ROCE and asset turnover.

5 **Discuss the implications of changes in the three ratios for the**
- **owners of the business**
- **the business's employees.**   **8 marks**

Assessment evidence: C5, A3, A4

 Look at each ratio and weigh up the changes that are taking place. Decide how they affect each group of stakeholders.

Answer

The owners of Pizza Express are the shareholders. The shareholders would look for an increase in the profit margin and ROCE because these are measures of profitability. The asset turnover measures sales revenue relative to net assets. It shows how effectively the assets are being used. Although this and the ROCE have gone down, it may be because the 40 new outlets have yet to reach their sales potential. Many shareholders understand this and will be interested in the long term financial health of the business. Their rewards will come in dividends from profits and from the share value increasing.

Earnings per share 1999	33.7p
Earnings per share 1998	26.7p

The earnings per share measures how much profit each share earns. They would look at this to compare rates of return from alternative investments, especially for similar businesses. They would want this figure to be high and to be improving as shown in the table above. It shows that the profit earned by each share has improved, but not all of it goes to the shareholders. Pizza Express will keep a sizable chunk of this for new investment. The chief executive's statement clearly emphasises the expansionary policy of the business. This means that dividends may be lower in the short term.

The employees will see things in a different light. The expansion of Pizza Express brings greater employment opportunities and makes their jobs more secure. Employees will not want the profit margins to increase if this means their wages not going up or working conditions deteriorating. The employees' unions may, in fact, use the increasing profit margin as evidence that their members are more productive and should receive a pay rise. The unions will compare Pizza Express with similar companies in the industry.

A business like Pizza Express may look at sales per square foot as a type of asset turnover ratio. This way it can check on the performance of individual outlets. Poorly performing restaurants will either have to improve, or risk closure.

Testing times: Edexcel

The following questions are adapted from Edexcel tests.

Assessment evidence	
E4	Identify appropriate financial information and use it to calculate performance, solvency and profitability ratios
C6	Compare and evaluate ratios in different businesses over time
C7	Explain how businesses manage their working capital
A4	Draw conclusions about the financial performance of the business based on your use and understanding of a range of financial data

How profitable is it? page 48 explains profit margins.

Is it solvent? page 50 explains current ratio.

Keeping close control page 52 explains acid test, stock turnover and debtor days.

What's the return? page 54 explains ROCE.

1 Use the data below to help you complete the shaded column headed 2000 on page 65. **8 marks**

Assessment evidence: E4

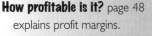 You will need to follow the advice and make calculations for average capital and average stock.

Look carefully at the dates. The capital is at 1/1/00, the beginning of the year. Since no new capital was injected into the business it follows that the capital at the end will be the same as the capital at the beginning minus any drawings and plus any new profit. It seems a complicated thing to ask you to do especially for the marks on offer. It's quite a high order skill and you will have to work hard to earn full marks in this question. The net assets = the closing capital.

	Year 2000
Credit sales	60 969
Gross profit	49 082
Net profit	7682
Capital at 1/1/00	53 526
Drawings	6000
Current assets	19 363
Current liabilities	9155
Stock at 1/1/2000	800
Stock at 31/12/2000	3913
Debtors	9700

- No long term liabilities and no additional capital was put into the business.

- Average capital $= \dfrac{(\text{opening capital} + \text{closing capital})}{2}$

- Average stock $= \dfrac{(\text{opening stock} + \text{closing stock})}{2}$

- You will need to derive some information from the data.

- Round your answers to two decimal places.

INTERPRETING FINANCIAL INFORMATION

The opening capital is £53 526.

The closing capital = opening capital, add net profit for the year,
take away the drawings from the business
= £53 526 + £7682 – £6000 = £55 208.

The average capital = (£53 526 + £55 208)/2 = £54 367.

The average stock = (£888 + £3913)/2 = £2356.50.

Ratio	Formula	1999	2000
Gross profit percentage (or margin)	$\dfrac{\text{Gross profit} \times 100}{\text{Sales revenue or turnover}}$	74.20%	80.50%
Net profit percentage	$\dfrac{\text{Net profit} \times 100}{\text{Sales revenue or turnover}}$	13.79%	12.60%
The ROCE	$\dfrac{\text{Net profit} \times 100}{\text{Average capital}}$	23.32%	14.13%
Current	$\dfrac{\text{Current assets}}{\text{Current liabilities}}$	1.16:1	2.12:1
Acid test	$\dfrac{\text{Current assets} - \text{stock}}{\text{Current liabilities}}$	0.88:1	1.69:1
Debtor days	$\dfrac{\text{Debtors} \times 365}{\text{Credit sales}}$	43.82 days	58.07 days
Stock turnover	$\dfrac{\text{Cost of sales}}{\text{Average stock held}}$	4.92 times a year	5.04 times a year
Asset turnover	$\dfrac{\text{Sales}}{\text{Net assets}}$	0.98:1	1.10:1

---

2   **Identify ALL the liquidity ratios and for each state whether
it has improved or declined from 1999 to 2000.**   **2 marks**

Assessment evidence: C6

Help!   You will need knowledge of the purpose of the ratios to answer this and an
understanding of whether a numerical increase is an improvement or a decline.

Answer

	1999	2000	
Current	1.16:1	2.12:1	Improved
Acid test	0.88:1	1.69:1	Improved

3 Analyse the liquidity of the business at the end of 1999. **2 marks**

Assessment evidence: A4

 Now use the ratios to explain the state of the business.

Answer

It would be useful to know what the normal liquidity is for this type of industry. The current ratio now means that for every £1 it owes it can find £1.16. It looks as if the business is solvent. However, a low stock turnover means it is not easy to turn stock into cash. It may be best to exclude stock from the calculations and therefore use the acid test ratio to check on solvency. Figure for the acid test ratio is below the desired 1:1. Using this ratio the business can raise 88.1p for every £1 of current liability. There is a risk of the business becoming insolvent. The management should closely monitor changes in this ratio.

4 Identify all profitability ratios and for each, state whether it has improved or declined from 1999 to 2000? **3 marks**

Assessment evidence: C6

 You will need knowledge of the purpose of the ratios to answer this and an understanding of whether a numerical increase is an improvement or a decline.

Answer

Ratio	1999	2000	
Gross profit percentage (or margin)	74.20%	80.50%	Improved
Net profit percentage	13.79%	12.60%	Declined
The ROCE	23.32%	14.13%	Declined

5 The management have decided to introduce Just in Time. Give reasons why they wish to do this, explaining how stock-holding costs would be reduced. **3 marks**

Assessment evidence: C7

Keeping the cash going
page 82 explains stock turnover.

 Check up on the relationship between the speed at which stock turns over and just-in-time.

Answer

JIT means receiving deliveries of stock only when the business is about to use them. This has three benefits. Being able to keep very low levels of stock would mean less money would be tied up in stock that might not be sold for some time. This would lower the working capital needs and reduce the cash outflow. The business would also need less space to hold stocks and wouldn't need to have so much staff time given over to looking after the stocks. It would save storage costs.

Testing times: OCR

The following questions are adapted from OCR tests.

<table>
<tr><th colspan="2">Assessment evidence</th></tr>
<tr><td>E4</td><td>Identify appropriate financial information and use it to calculate performance, solvency and profitability ratios</td></tr>
<tr><td>C2</td><td>Explain why different groups of stakeholders may interpret data about the financial performance of a business in different ways</td></tr>
<tr><td>C5</td><td>Explain how financial ratios are used by different groups of stakeholders to interpret financial data</td></tr>
<tr><td>C6</td><td>Compare and evaluate ratios in different businesses over time</td></tr>
<tr><td>A2</td><td>Evaluate the significance of the final accounts to different groups of stakeholders</td></tr>
<tr><td>A3</td><td>Explain why ratios change over time and how this affects different groups of stakeholders</td></tr>
<tr><td>A4</td><td>Draw conclusions about the financial performance of the business based on your use and understanding of a range of financial data</td></tr>
</table>

Fresh Ideas Ltd, a publishing company, wishes to publish more materials in the CD Rom format. It wants to subcontract production of its CD to CD Productions Ltd. However, CD Productions Ltd want to inspect some of Fresh Ideas Ltd's financial records to see if they are a good company.

1 **Using the figures for both years, select and calculate four appropriate ratios for each year (use the same type of ratio for both years for comparison).** **8 marks**

Assessment evidence: E4

Fresh Ideas Ltd trading profit & loss account	Year ending 31 December 2000		Year ending 31 December 1999	
	£	£	£	£
Turnover		110 000		100 000
Opening stock	12 000		8500	
Purchases	55 050		62 000	
Total	67 050		70 500	
Closing stock	(15 000)		(12 000)	
Cost of goods sold		52 050		58 500
Gross profit		57 950		41 500
Expenses	43 000		41 300	
Total		43 000		41 300
Net profit		14 950		200

(Data continued overleaf.)

Fresh Ideas Ltd balance sheet	31 December 2000		31 December 1999	
	£	£	£	£
Fixed assets				
Buildings at net book value	50 000		50 000	
Plant and machinery at nbv	80 000		82 000	
Vehicles at nbv	30 000		32 000	
Total		160 000		164 000
Current assets				
Stock	15 000		12 000	
Debtors	25 000		11 300	
Bank	1 200		750	
Cash	250		450	
Total		41 450		24 500
Current liabilities				
Creditors	30 000		32 000	
Total		(30 000)		32 000
Working capital (net current assets)		11 450		–7 500
Net assets		171 450		156 500
Financed by				
Capital	160 000		160 000	
Retained profit	21 450		6 500	
Total		181 450		166 500
Less drawings	(10 000)		10 000	
Net worth		171 450		156 500

Ratios in a nutshell page 86.
Ratios are dealt with in detail on pages 48–58.

Help! All the ratios are given here. Some have been left for you to practise the workings.

Ratio	Formula	Type of ratio	Who might use them	2000	1999
Net profit margin	$\dfrac{\text{Net profit} \times 100}{\text{Sales revenue or turnover}}$	Profitability	Owners, investors, banks, managers, competitors	(£14 950/110 000) x 100 = 13.6%	(200/100 000) x 100 = 0.2%
The ROCE	$\dfrac{\text{Net (or operating) profit} \times 100}{\text{Capital employed}}$	Profitability	Owners, investors, banks, managers, employees, trade unions, competitors	(14 950/171 450) x 100 = 8.7%	You complete the workings 0.1%
Current ratio	$\dfrac{\text{Current assets}}{\text{Current liabilities}}$	Liquidity or solvency	Banks, creditors, managers	41 450 : 30 000 30 000 : 30 000 1.38 : 1	You complete the workings 0.77:1
Acid test ratio	$\dfrac{\text{Current assets} - \text{stock}}{\text{Current liabilities}}$	Liquidity or solvency	Banks, creditors	41 450 – 15 000 : 30 000 30 000 : 30 000 0.88 : 1	You complete the workings 0.39 : 1
Asset turnover	$\dfrac{\text{Sales}}{\text{Net assets}}$	Efficiency or performance	Managers, owners, investors	110 000 171 450 0.64 times	You complete the workings 0.64 times
Debtor days	$\dfrac{\text{Debtors} \times 365}{\text{Credit sales}}$	Efficiency or performance	Managers	25 000 x 365 110 000 83 days	You complete the workings 41 days
Creditor days	$\dfrac{\text{Creditors} \times 365}{\text{Credit purchases (or cost of sales)}}$	Efficiency or performance	Managers	30 000 x 365 52 050 210 days	You complete the workings 200 days
Stock turnover	$\dfrac{\text{Cost of sales}}{\text{Average stock held}}$	Efficiency or performance	Managers	52 050 (12 000 + 15 000)/2 3.9 times	You complete the workings 5.7 times

2 Compare the ratios you have calculated and explain the significance of the results for CD Productions Ltd's investigation into Fresh Ideas Ltd.

4 marks

Assessment evidence: C5, C6

Help! See last question.

Answer

	Year 2000	Year 1999
Net profit margin	13.6%	0.2%
ROCE	8.7%	0.1%
Current ratio	1.38:1	0.77:1
Acid test	0.88:1	0.39:1
Asset turnover	64 times	64 times
Debtor days	83 days	41 days
Creditor days	210 days	200 days
Stock turnover	3.9 times	5.7 times

The net profit margin has increased from a very low 0.2% to 13.6% in 2000. This means that the business made a net profit of 13.6p for every £ of goods sold. It is a big improvement.

The ROCE has also improved dramatically from a poor 0.1% to a respectable 8.7% making it a more attractive investment.

The current ratio now means that for every £1 it owes it can find £1.38. The year before the ratio was well below 1:1 making the business at risk from insolvency.

The stock turnover rate has fallen to 3.9 times a year. A low stock turnover means it is not easy to turn stock into cash. It may be best to use the acid test ratio to check on solvency. Figures for both ratios are below 1:1, although the situation has improved significantly.

The asset turnover measures sales revenue relative to net assets. It shows how effectively the assets are being used. The figure has remained the same, meaning the business has not improved efficiency.

Unfortunately the debtor days have doubled suggesting the business is not efficient in collecting debts. The creditor days has seen a small increase. The business is not good at settling debts, especially if the trade credit period is 28 days.

3 Explain possible circumstances that may have caused the calculated ratios to change over the two year period.

4 marks

Assessment evidence: A3

Help! See last question.

Answer

The net profit margin may have increased because sales were up and cost of sales down. The business will have found cheaper suppliers. The small increase in expenses was much less than the increase in sales.

The improvement in the ROCE was due to the big increase in net profit from a pitiful £200 to nearly £15 000.

The improvement in the current ratio was down to a big increase in current assets and a small decrease in current liabilities making the working capital a positive figure.

The improvement in the acid test ratio was down to the big increase in debtors perhaps suggesting a healthier order book. However the acid test ratio remains below 1:1 so there is still a solvency problem.

The asset turnover has remained the same, even with depreciation making the fixed assets worth less.

The debtor days have increased suggesting some problem with the sales accounts department. Maybe poor monitoring through a change in staff. Better training and an aged debtors' list is required.

The creditor days have worsened. Better training is required to avoid upsetting the suppliers. It is also important to monitor the aged creditors' list.

---

4 **What conclusions can be drawn about the financial performance of Fresh Ideas Ltd? Explain how much importance CD Productions Ltd should place on the results of ratio analysis in making any decisions. What other factors should also be considered?** **10 marks**

Assessment evidence: C2, A4

Help! See last question.

Answer

There has been an overall improvement in the financial performance of Fresh Ideas Ltd in most areas. It is more profitable than before in terms of its ROCE and net profit margin. The risk of the business becoming insolvent has decreased, but it still has an acid test ratio below 1:1. This is the better ratio to use for Fresh Ideas Ltd as the rate of stock turnover is low at around 4.6 times a year. The stock turnover figure has fallen, suggesting it is shifting stock more slowly. It may pay Fresh Ideas Ltd to look at its stock control to see if it can reduce stock levels. Would JIT be an option?

Fresh Ideas Ltd might also improve both its debtor collection and creditor payment days. Unless the credit days are generous, these are both poor and are signs of inefficiency. Failure to collect debts on time might lead to a cash flow problem and may explain why Fresh Ideas Ltd is late in paying bills. It would be important to know if it has lost any suppliers because of this and how credit-worthy current suppliers think Fresh Ideas Ltd is. It would be useful to see the cash flow forecast and actual cash flows over the past year, especially as there is no overdraft shown on the balance sheet.

It might also pay to look at the share price and earnings per share to see how the shareholders view the business.

Testing times: practice questions

A Touch Of Glass is a small business making hand blown glass. An accountant was employed to put together the final accounts in the same style as the 1999 accounts.

A Touch Of Glass profit & loss account	Year ending 31 December 2000 £	Year ending 31 December 2000 £	Year ending 31 December 1999 £	Year ending 31 December 1999 £
Turnover		100 000		90 000
Opening stock	12 000		6 000	
Purchases	45 000		42 000	
Total	57 000		48 000	
Closing stock	(3 000)		(12 000)	
Cost of goods sold		54 000		36 000
Gross profit		46 000		54 000
Expenses	42 000		44 000	
Total		42 000		44 000
Net profit		4 000		10 000

A Touch of Glass balance sheet	31 December 2000 £	31 December 2000 £	31 December 1999 £	31 December 1999 £
Fixed assets				
Buildings at net book value	45 000		40 400	
Plant and machinery at nbv	56 000		60 000	
Total		101 000		100 400
Current assets				
Stock	3 000		12 000	
Debtors	9 000		8 000	
Bank	1 500		2 000	
Cash	900		600	
Total		14 400		22 600
Current liabilities				
Creditors	8 400		15 000	
Total		(8 400)		(15 000)
Working capital (net current assets)		6 000		7 600
Net assets		107 000		108 000
Financed by				
Capital	100 000		100 000	
Retained profit	12 000		16 600	
Total		112 000		116 600
Less drawings	5 000		8 600	
Net worth		107 000		108 000

1 What has happened to the value of the fixed assets of the business?

2 What has happened to the value of the net assets of the business?

3 Calculate the following ratios: net profit margin, gross profit margin, ROCE, current ratio, acid test ratio, asset turnover, debtor days, creditor days, stock turnover.

4 How happy are the creditors likely to be with the performance of the business in 2000 over that in 1999?

5 Why might the owner have taken less drawings out of the business in 2000?

6 Use ratios to support your views on the changes in the profitability performance of the business.

7 What has been the main cause of the change in profitability?

8 What solution might the manager put forward to improve the profitability of the business?

9 How efficient is the business in paying its debts?

10 The working capital needed to keep the business going has declined by about three times since the business has cut its stock levels. What effect has this had on its solvency ratios? Why might the bank wish to monitor changes in solvency levels?

11 How well has the business been shifting its stock in 2000 compared with 1999? What might have led to this change?

Why budget?

You need to know how budgets help planning, set targets and help control expenditure.

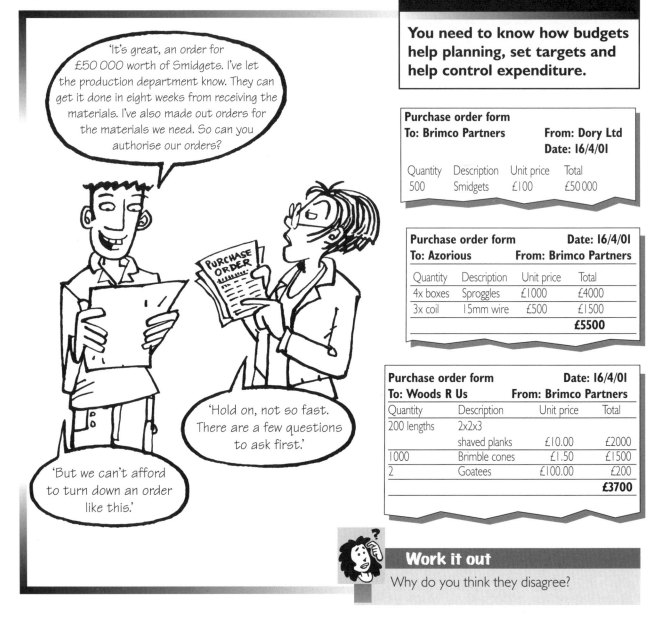

'It's great, an order for £50 000 worth of Smidgets. I've let the production department know. They can get it done in eight weeks from receiving the materials. I've also made out orders for the materials we need. So can you authorise our orders?'

'Hold on, not so fast. There are a few questions to ask first.'

'But we can't afford to turn down an order like this.'

Purchase order form
To: Brimco Partners   **From: Dory Ltd**
                                   Date: 16/4/01

Quantity	Description	Unit price	Total
500	Smidgets	£100	£50 000

Purchase order form   **Date: 16/4/01**
To: Azorious   **From: Brimco Partners**

Quantity	Description	Unit price	Total
4x boxes	Sproggles	£1000	£4000
3x coil	15mm wire	£500	£1500
			£5500

Purchase order form   **Date: 16/4/01**
To: Woods R Us   **From: Brimco Partners**

Quantity	Description	Unit price	Total
200 lengths	2x2x3 shaved planks	£10.00	£2000
1000	Brimble cones	£1.50	£1500
2	Goatees	£100.00	£200
			£3700

Why do you think they disagree?

BUT CAN WE AFFORD TO ACCEPT IT?

Both managers at Brimco have good points. Orders help you make profits, but will the business have enough money to cover all the bills and expenses? They decided to do a few sums and make a budget.

- Order received mid April.
- Order materials mid April.
- Receive materials end of April. Start the eight week production 1 May.
- Pay for materials end of May.
- Pay wages, expenses, power 29th of each month.
- Deliver Smidgets end of June.
- Receive payments end of July.

To fulfil the order

	Date payable	Cost	Total cost
Raw materials	30 May	£9200	£9200
Power	per month	£400	£800
Wages	per month	£9000	£18 000
Expenses	per month	£6000	£12 000
		Total cost	£40 000

Plenty of cash is going out before any is coming in

Money in		Date		Money out	Cumulative money out
	Order received mid April	16 April	Order materials		
		30 April	Receive materials end of April		
	Start the eight week production	1 May			
		29 May	Pay wages, overheads, power	£15 400	£15 400
		30 May	Pay for materials	£9200	£24 600
	Finish production	29 June	Pay wages, overheads, power	£15 400	£40 000
	Deliver goods	30 June			
£50 000	Receive payments	30 July			

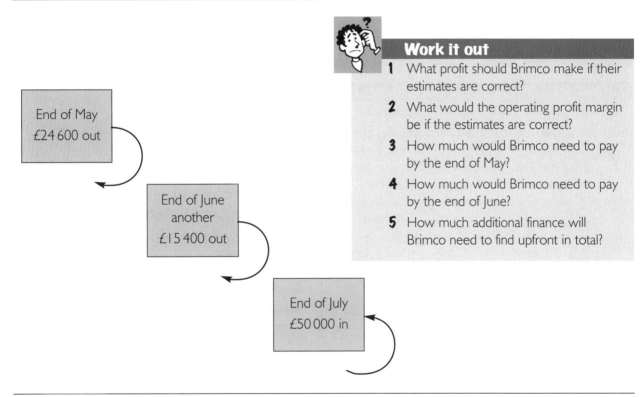

End of May
£24 600 out

End of June
another
£15 400 out

End of July
£50 000 in

Work it out

1 What profit should Brimco make if their estimates are correct?

2 What would the operating profit margin be if the estimates are correct?

3 How much would Brimco need to pay by the end of May?

4 How much would Brimco need to pay by the end of June?

5 How much additional finance will Brimco need to find upfront in total?

WHAT DOES THE BUSINESS NEED TO DO?

By making some calculations, Brimco is planning its cash needs and the timing of these needs. Once the business knows its cash requirements it will need to make arrangements to cover them. It would be unwise to accept the order before these arrangements are in place.

- Brimco would look at the cash it has available and whether it needs to take out an overdraft to cover the shortfall.

- Brimco might try to arrange for the stock to be delivered in two batches. This would delay payment on the second batch until the end of June.

- Brimco could ask for 56 days credit.

To help it make these decisions Brimco would produce a budget. This is a short term financial plan. The one shown in the table above is a simple version. More needs to be added to it such as where the money will come from to pay the bills due.

As part of this budget Brimco would produce a cash flow forecast. The bank would certainly insist on seeing the cash flow forecast before considering whether to offer an overdraft.

The **cash flow forecast** is exactly what is says – a forecast of the cash going out and coming into the business. It is therefore made up from estimates. The more accurate the estimates the better the forecast. If the business has had similar orders in the past it will use these to help it make more accurate estimates.

Building a budget...

HOW TO CONSTRUCT A BUDGET AND CASH FLOW FORECAST

Samantha was a former Welsh international in netball and CDT teacher until her break from the job to be a mother. She always wanted to be her own boss. Samantha had an idea that she could produce a range of alternative sports trophies whose originality would command a premium price and compete easily with the bland gold and silver trophies on plastic plinths, which currently adorned her mantle-shelf. Samantha Beale comes to visit Rahel at Facts and Figures for advice.

Small business advice from Facts and Figures

Do you need help with
- Budgets • Cash flow
- Sorting out your accounts?

Contact Facts and Figures for the best independent advice at prices you can afford.

'I want to set up my own business called Alternative Sports Trophies and I want some advice with the cash flow and budget part of my business plan. I've done some research.

I need two machines to help me cut and shape the trophies. These **two machines** would cost £1500. I can purchase second-hand **office furniture** for £1000 and a new **computer** with software and a printer for £1600 with a year's on-site warranty. It all seems a lot of money to pay out.

My raw materials are quite cheap, being metal wire, hardwood cut offs, old broken sports gear, paints, cardboard packaging and odds and ends. I reckon that £90 per month should cover **raw materials**. I'll need to **employ one worker and one part time secretary** at a total wage bill of £1300 per month and I want to pay myself a **salary** of £1200 per month.

Postage would be on average 50p per trophy. Oh

yes, and other costs include £350 **insurance fee** payable in April. **Advertising** in the trade press would be heaviest at the beginning. I've decided to spend £60 in the first two months, then reduce this to £20 per month. **Telephone bills** would be £80 payable every three months. **Other overheads** including energy would be about £120 a month.

I'm concerned that the business is seasonal. The main sales will be in the early part of the year, for winter sports trophies, and then a smaller peak in July and August for the end of the summer season. I've done some research and **predicted sales** for a six-month period. Each **trophy will sell for £8.50** including postage and packaging.

I have a small inheritance of £2700 I can invest (**owner's capital**). I've found a place to **rent** for £400 per month. It is a small unit underneath the railway arches. I will need to **borrow funds**. How much and what is the interest?'

Work it out

1 What does Samantha need to consider when setting up her business?

2 Why is it important to produce a realistic budget?

3 How does a cash flow forecast contribute to her thinking?

Facts and Figures explained that the **consultancy fee** will be £600 payable during the first month's trading.

- The **capital budget** includes the assets Samantha will buy to produce the trophies.

- The **cash budget** includes payments for invoices and expenses as well as receipts.

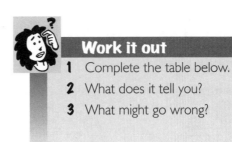

Work it out

1 Complete the table below.

2 What does it tell you?

3 What might go wrong?

Samantha's budget

	Capital expenditure	Revenue expenditure	Frequency of payments
Two machines	Yes		One off
Office furniture			
Computer			
Raw materials			
Postage and packaging			
Wages			
Salary		Yes	Monthly
Insurance fee			
Advertising			
Telephone			
Other overheads			
Rent			
Loan interest			
Consultancy fee			

Revenue expenditure means expenditure on everyday running costs of a business.

Capital expenditure means the expenditure spent on the fixed assets

WORKING OUT THE BUDGET

The budget and the cash flow forecast interact. In building a budget, a business tries out its plans by feeding 'what ifs' into the cash flow spreadsheet.

- Will that big order mean that the creditors are knocking at the door?

- Will adding another employee cause financial difficulties?

- Will extending the factory mean that we will do better because we can produce more?

- What is the effect of updating the computer system?

The answers from the cash flow forecast will then be fed back into the budget until a working conclusion is reached. Of course, much of it depends on estimates, so making them as accurate as possible is very important.

...and forecasting cash flow

What's it all about?

You need to be able to identify and interpret variance and explain the benefits of budgeting to businesses.

Work it out

1 Samantha and Rahel have dealt with all the expenditure in the budget. What do they need to do now?

2 Why is this more difficult?

3 Why is it important to be as accurate as possible?

WILL THE CASH FLOW?

Rahel has drawn up a cash flow forecast for Samantha before they meet again. She identified some factors which Sam needed to take into consideration. Rahel took the cash flow forecast to the meeting and explained the options to Samantha.

First cash flow forecast for Alternative Sports Trophies drawn up by Facts and Figures

Sales numbers	350	400	400	550	600	450	2750
Money coming in	April	May	June	July	August	September	Totals
Owner's capital	2700.00						2700.00
Loan	0.00						0.00
Sales revenue	2975.00	3400.00	3400.00	4675.00	5100.00	3825.00	23 375.00
Total receipts	**5675.00**	**3400.00**	**3400.00**	**4675.00**	**5100.00**	**3825.00**	**26 075.00**
							0.00
Money flowing out							0.00
Rent of premises	400.00	400.00	400.00	400.00	400.00	400.00	2400.00
Machines	1500.00						1500.00
Loan repayment	0.00	0.00	0.00	0.00	0.00	0.00	0.00
Samantha's salary	1200.00	1200.00	1200.00	1200.00	1200.00	1200.00	7200.00
Office furniture	1000.00						1000.00
Computer	1600.00						1600.00
Wages	1300.00	1300.00	1300.00	1300.00	1300.00	1300.00	7800.00
Raw materials	90.00	90.00	90.00	90.00	90.00	90.00	540.00
Advertising	60.00	60.00	20.00	20.00	20.00	20.00	200.00
Consultancy fee	600.00						600.00
Telephone			80.00			80.00	160.00
Postage & packaging	175.00	200.00	200.00	275.00	300.00	225.00	1375.00
Insurance	350.00						350.00
Other overheads	120.00	120.00	120.00	120.00	120.00	120.00	720.00
Total payments	**8395.00**	**3370.00**	**3410.00**	**3405.00**	**3430.00**	**3435.00**	**25 445.00**
Net cash flow	−2720.00	30.00	−10.00	1270.00	1670.00	390.00	
Add opening balance	0.00	−2720.00	−2690.00	−2700.00	−1430.00	240.00	
Closing balance	**−2720.00**	**−2690.00**	**−2700.00**	**−1430.00**	**240.00**	**630.00**	

No loan decided yet.

Can Sam do with less salary in the first few months?

Total sales may be an over-estimate or an underestimate.

Work it out

Look at the cash flow forecast, Rahel's comments and the graph.

1 How much cash is she short by?

2 Look at Rahel's comments. What would you recommend Samantha do?

WHAT CHANGES?

Rahel recommended that Samantha:

- draws out £200 less salary in the first three months;

- pays for the computer by instalments;

- takes out a loan to cover the shortfall.

This would provide Samantha with a reserve, should sales be more sluggish than she estimated.

First cash flow forecast

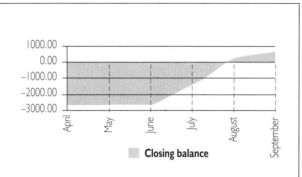

Money coming in	April	May	June	July	August	September	Totals
Owner's capital	2700.00						2700.00
Loan	2500.00						2500.00
Sales revenue	2975.00	3400.00	3400.00	4675.00	5100.00	3825.00	23 375.00
Total receipts	8175.00	3400.00	3400.00	4675.00	5100.00	3825.00	28 575.00
Money flowing out							
Rent of premises	400.00	400.00	400.00	400.00	400.00	400.00	2400.00
Machines	1500.00						1500.00
Loan repayment	100.00	100.00	100.00	100.00	100.00	100.00	600.00
Samantha's salary	1000.00	1000.00	1000.00	1200.00	1200.00	1200.00	6600.00
Office furniture	1000.00						1000.00
Computer	420.00	420.00	420.00	420.00			1680.00
Wages	1300.00	1300.00	1300.00	1300.00	1300.00	1300.00	7800.00
Raw materials	90.00	90.00	90.00	90.00	90.00	90.00	540.00
Advertising	60.00	60.00	20.00	20.00	20.00	20.00	200.00
Consultancy fee	600.00						600.00
Telephone			80.00			80.00	160.00
Postage & packaging	175.00	200.00	200.00	275.00	300.00	225.00	1375.00
Insurance	350.00						350.00
Other overheads	120.00	120.00	120.00	120.00	120.00	120.00	720.00
Total payments	7115.00	3690.00	3730.00	3925.00	3530.00	3535.00	25 525.00
Net cash flow	1060.00	−290.00	−330.00	750.00	1570.00	290.00	
Add opening balance	0.00	1060.00	770.00	440.00	1190.00	2760.00	
Closing balance	1060.00	770.00	440.00	1190.00	2760.00	3050.00	

Work it out

1 What effect did Rahel's recommendation have on the cash flow?

2 Has she enough cash to pay the bills?

3 In which month is the closing balance the lowest?

GOING AHEAD?

After the meeting, Samantha went home to think about it all. She had always wanted to be a teacher, but the thought of running her own business was very tempting. Just think about the independence – but what about the risk? Teaching wasn't as secure as it used to be but would people really buy her trophies?

She'd already done some market research and the prospects looked good. Just think, if it really worked, she could even run a specialist line of personalised trophies. Sports clubs always liked to reward special members in ways they would never forget. She decided to go for it.

Let's find out what happened...

Right or wrong?

What's it all about?

You need to be able to identify and interpret variance, and explain the benefits of budgeting to businesses.

Work it out

1 Why do you think Samantha and Rahel are looking gloomy?

2 What might be the cause of their problems?

GETTING IT WRONG?

Samantha, who owns and runs Alternative Sports Trophies, went along, in a gloomy mood, to her June meeting with Rahel from Facts and Figures. Samantha's sales for the first two months had been much lower than she estimated. Rahel looked closely at the actual cash flow and compared it with the budget. She marked the differences or **variances** on the cash flow.

Work it out

1 By how much had she overestimated the value of sales for each month?

2 What were the changes between the budget and the actual costs and revenue?

3 Why would she be disappointed with these figures?

4 Could she have done anything to make her estimates more accurate?

Money coming in	Actual April	Forecast April	Variance April	Actual May	Forecast May	Variance May
Owner's capital	2700.00	2700.00	0.00			0.00
Loan	2500.00	2500.00	0.00			0.00
Sales revenue	2040.00	2975.00	−935.00	3230.00	3400.00	−170.00
Total receipts	7240.00	8175.00	−935.00	3230.00	3400.00	−170.00
Money flowing out						
Rent of premises	400.00	400.00	0.00	400.00	400.00	0.00
Machines	1500.00	1500.00	0.00			
Loan repayment	100.00	100.00	0.00	100.00	100.00	0.00
Samantha's salary	1000.00	1000.00	0.00	1000.00	1000.00	0.00
Office furniture	1000.00	1000.00	0.00			
Computer	420.00	420.00	0.00	420.00	420.00	0.00
Wages	1300.00	1300.00	0.00	1300.00	1300.00	0.00
Raw materials	60.00	90.00	−30.00	85.00	90.00	−5.00
Advertising	60.00	60.00	0.00	100.00	60.00	40.00
Consultancy fee	600.00	600.00	0.00			
Postage & packaging	120.00	175.00	−55.00	190.00	200.00	−10.00
Insurance	350.00	350.00	0.00			
Other overheads	120.00	120.00	0.00	120.00	120.00	0.00
Total payments	7030.00	7115.00	−85.00	3715.00	3690.00	25.00
Net cash flow	210.00	1060.00	−850.00	−485.00	−290.00	−195.00
Add opening balance	0.00	0.00	0.00	210.00	1060.00	−850.00
Closing balance	210.00	1060.00	−850.00	−275.00	770.00	−1045.00

HOW DOES IT VARY?

A variance is the difference between the budget and what actually happens. The budget is the target for the business.

Adverse variance	Favourable variance
Sales revenue (sales turnover) is less than the amount in the budget.	Sales revenue (sales turnover) is greater than the amount in the budget.
Actual expenditure (costs) is greater than the amount in the budget.	Actual expenditure (costs) is less than the amount in the budget.

In the tables below:

A = Adverse

F = Favourable

WHAT ABOUT SAMANTHA'S BUDGET?

Rahel noted down that:

■ sales were £1105 down for the first two months;

■ costs had only been reduced by £85 in April and had risen by £25 in May making a net reduction of only £60;

■ Samantha has £1045 less cash than she had budgeted for.

Profit and loss for the first two months trading

	Actual	Forecast	Variance	
Sales revenue	5270	6375	–1105	A
Cost of sales	145	180	–35	F
Gross profit	5125	6195	–1070	A
Expenses	6416	6441	–25	F
Net profit	–1291	–246	–1045	A

■ Cost of sales refers to the cost of the raw materials.

Samantha's bank manager phoned to tell her she was overdrawn by £275. He wanted to see her.

Samantha had decided to increase advertising in May. She also trailed around sports shops and clubs with her samples. At least sales were going up.

Work it out

1 What profit or loss did Samantha expect to have after two months' trading?

2 What was the actual loss after two months' trading?

3 What could Samantha do?

4 Explain these changes in terms of favourable and unfavourable variances.

Variances can be measured for any budget heading. Look at the table below

Time period	Actual	Budget	Variance	
Labour costs	£12 000	£10 000	£2000	A
Stock	£5890	£6500	–£610	F

The business has used less stock. This is a favourable variance. There might have been less wastage or a cheaper supplier was found. The adverse variance in labour costs might have been due to underestimating the labour needs for the job. It might have been the first time the business had taken on this type of order.

Fixed overheads include the rent, wages of salaried staff and other resources that do not change when production falls or rises. These are often easier to estimate because they are set in advance. **Variable overheads**, which change as output changes, are harder to get right. The commission paid to sales representatives will rise if sales rise.

Keeping the cash going

What's it all about?

You need to know how businesses control their working capital and manage their cash to solve cash flow problems.

The secret of keeping the cash going is to make sure you are using your working capital efficiently.

Working capital is really the net current assets shown on the balance sheet. The net current assets are the current assets minus the current liabilities (see page 27). The working capital is really like a cash merry-go-round.

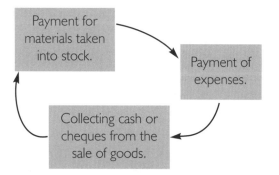

The idea is to make your working capital work harder for you by reducing the time taken between paying for your stock and receiving money or cheques from your sales. This speeds up the cycle. The faster the cycle the less working capital needs to be financed from other sources.

Work it out

Jo is anxious about the state of her bank account. How might she improve the state of her working capital and cash flow?

Rate of stock turnover shows how many times batches of stock were sold during the last accounting period. It measures the speed that the stock is moved on.

$$\text{rate of stock turnover} = \frac{\text{cost of sales}}{\text{average stock}}$$

Part of Jo's Diner trading account

Turnover (sales revenue)		110 000
Cost of sales		
Opening stock	0	
Purchases	62 000	
Subtotal	62 000	
Closing stock	10 000	
Cost of sales		52 000

The cost of sales is £52 000.

The average stock held is the opening stock added on to the closing stock divided by 2.

Rate of stock turnover = 52 000/5000 = 10.4 times a year, or 365/10.4 = 35 days.

Stock held by the business is tying up cash. A business pays for stock from suppliers and then spends money converting the stock into goods. Any stock lying around, whether as raw materials, partly completed goods (**work in progress**) or finished goods, is not earning the business money. Instead, money has been tied up in these. A more rapid turnover of stock would release this money.

Part of Jo's Diner trading account one year later

Turnover (sales revenue)		130000
Cost of sales		
Opening stock	10000	
Purchases	67000	
Subtotal	77000	
Closing stock	3000	
Cost of sales		74000

Work it out

1 Calculate the rate of stock turnover in both times – per year – and days.
2 Has the rate improved?
3 If Jo had decided to reduce stock levels early on in the year she would be able to say that the average stock held would be nearer the £3000. What would the new rate of stock turnover be?

Imagine being able to keep very low levels of stock that you would top up when required. Less money would be tied up in stock. The business would need less space to hold stocks and would receive deliveries only when needed. This method of stock control is called **Just in Time**. It relies on the supplier guaranteeing the delivery. Computers link suppliers and customers to enable orders to be placed when stocks are required.

The **debtors' collection period** or **debtor days** is a ratio that measures the average time debtors take to pay their outstanding balances (see page 53). It is better if the debtor days get shorter than longer.

debtors' collection period = debtors x 365 days divided by credit sales

Credit sales for the year	£28000
Debtors at the end of the year as shown on the balance sheet	£3000

Debtors' collection period

$$= \frac{3000 \times 365}{28000} = 39 \text{ days}$$

Creditors' payment days (also known as **creditor days**) measures the average number of days it takes a business to pay its creditors. A longer period improves the cash flow of the business; however, a business may upset its suppliers if it delays payments too long and gets a bad reputation and even becomes a bad credit risk. Using IT to automate payments would help improve the image of the business.

$$\text{creditors' payment period} = \frac{\text{creditors} \times 365}{\text{credit purchases}}$$

Jo's Diner	
Creditors as recorded on the balance sheet	£8500
Credit purchases in the financial year	£52000

Work it out

1 Calculate the creditors' payment days.
2 The business usually has 30 days' credit with its suppliers. What would you advise the business to do given its creditor payment period figures?

Keeping the wolf from the door

What's it all about?

You need to know how businesses use estimates to set targets and later check their performance against these.

KEEPING OUT OF TROUBLE

Businesses are often started by people with a bright idea who may not have the necessary financial expertise.

Did you know the following facts?

- Seven out of ten new businesses fail to survive the first year because of cash flow problems.

- A profitable business can easily run out of cash if it accepts orders without finding out where the cash will come from.

- A cash flow forecast is only as good as the estimates.

CASH FLOW IS CRUCIAL

When cash flow goes wrong, it may be the beginning of the end. Many aspects of cash flow are fundamental to the running of the business.

- A business should set targets for sales and monitor its forecasts against the actual sales.

- The cash flow forecast can be used to check on business spending.

- The cash flow forecast will support applications for loans and overdrafts.

Work it out

1 What will probably happen when the creditors are knocking on the door?

2 Make a list of the financial processes that a business needs to keep under control to avoid having problems with its creditors.

3 If a business hits trouble, what should it try to do?

It can also be used to help recognise opportunities and changes that can be made to the activities of the business.

Many businesses, especially seasonal ones, use cash flow forecasts to recognise quiet periods and make plans. A hotel might put on special events for winter weekends.

WATCHING THE BUDGET

Cash flow often goes wrong because budgets were unrealistic. An enthusiastic entrepreneur can easily be optimistic about sales, so it's important to estimate as accurately as possible. The next step is to work out the variances.

Remember Hatrick? Here is one of its job cards.

Job 88	Budgeted use	Budgeted price/rate	Total budget cost	Actual usage	Actual price/ rate	Actual cost	Variance	Favourable/ adverse
Labour	20 hours	£5 per hour	£100.00	18 hours	£5 per hour	£90.00	−£10.00	Favourable
Materials	10m	£8.9 per metre	£89.00	12m	£8.9 per metre	£106.80	£17.80	Adverse
Overheads	3 hours	£10 per hour	£30.00	3 hours	£10 per hour	£30.00	£0	~

Work it out

1 What was the total variance?

2 Was it favourable or adverse?

3 Why might Hatrick have used more materials than it estimated?

4 Why might Hatrick have overestimated the labour needs?

RATIOS CAN HELP AS WELL

A business that wants to make the money move more quickly needs to look at:

- rate of stock turnover;
- debtor payment days;
- creditor payment days.

Bringing all three ratios together will show how long it takes from the moment the stock is paid for to the moment money comes in from sales. This is called the **working capital cycle**.

Speeding up the cycle	Ratio
■ Reduce the levels of stock held, by getting deliveries only when you really need them	■ Rate of stock turnover
■ Take longer to pay creditors	■ Debtor payment days
■ Speed up the rate debtors pay	■ Creditor payment days

To work out what's going on:

Rate of stock turnover + debtor days − creditor days

44 days + 39 days − 41 days = 42 days.

A business wants this figure to fall if working capital is to circulate more quickly.

	Year 2000	2001
Rate of stock turnover	25	21
Debtor days	33	30
Creditor days	35	35

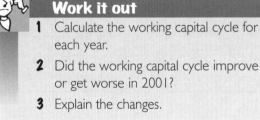

Work it out

1 Calculate the working capital cycle for each year.

2 Did the working capital cycle improve or get worse in 2001?

3 Explain the changes.

WINNING THE GAME

Finance isn't just a chore! It can help to control, guide and influence the activities of a business. Keeping a check list of the financial processes helps to focus the mind on what must be done and what must be watched.

In the end a business cannot function unless its financial records are kept efficiently. A company that does not submit its accounts will in the end be struck off the register of companies!

Ratios in a nutshell

What's it all about?

You need to be able to look at a summary of all the key ratios and be able to identify who is most interested in each.

Ratio or performance indicator	Formula	Type of ratio	Who might use them (Stakeholders)	Which accounts to use or where to find the information	Page
ROCE	$\dfrac{\text{Net (or operating) profit} \times 100}{\text{Capital employed}}$	Profitability	Owners, investors, banks, managers, competitors	Balance sheet, profit and loss	54
Gross profit margin	$\dfrac{\text{Gross profit} \times 100}{\text{Sales revenue or turnover}}$	Profitability	Owners, investors, banks, managers, employees and trade unions, competitors	Profit and loss	49
Net profit margin (operating profit margin)	$\dfrac{\text{Net (or operating) profit} \times 100}{\text{Sales revenue or turnover}}$	Profitability	Owners, investors, banks, managers, employees and trade unions, competitors	Profit and loss	48
Current ratio	$\dfrac{\text{Current assets}}{\text{Current liabilities}}$	Liquidity or solvency	Banks, creditors, managers	Balance sheet	51
Acid test ratio	$\dfrac{\text{Current assets} - \text{stock}}{\text{Current liabilities}}$	Liquidity or solvency	Banks, creditors	Balance sheet	52
Asset turnover	$\dfrac{\text{Sales}}{\text{Net assets}}$	Efficiency or performance	Managers, owners, investors	Profit and loss and balance sheet	55
Debtor days	$\dfrac{\text{Debtors} \times 365}{\text{Credit sales}}$	Efficiency or performance	Managers	Balance sheet, profit and loss	53, 83
Creditor days	$\dfrac{\text{Creditors} \times 365}{\text{Credit purchases}}$	Efficiency or performance	Managers	Balance sheet, profit and loss	83
Stock turnover	$\dfrac{\text{Cost of sales}}{\text{Average stock held}}$	Efficiency or performance	Managers	Profit and loss	52, 82
Earnings per share	$\dfrac{\text{Profit after tax}}{\text{Number of issued shares}}$	Stockholder returns	Owners, potential investors, competitors	Financial papers, Company internet sites, Annual Reports	59 59
Price earnings ratio	$\dfrac{\text{Current market price of a share}}{\text{Earnings per share}}$	Stockholder returns	Owners, potential investors, competitors	Financial papers, Company internet sites, Annual Reports	59 59

WHAT TO LOOK FOR IN RATIOS

- Look for trends over years.

- Compare similar businesses.

- Compare a business with the average results of similar businesses.

Ratios can be expressed as a ratio or as a percentage or as a time period.

ROCE measures how efficiently the capital is working for the business in terms of making profits. An alternative use of the capital would have been to put the money in a bank, so it is worth comparing ROCE with interest on savings. ROCE should be higher.

Gross profit margin measures the business's gross profit as a percentage of sales or turnover. The gross profit margin will improve if the business can buy cheaper supplies or it can raise prices.

Net profit margin measures the business's net profit as a percentage of sales or turnover. It tells the business how much the business earns for every £1 of sales after paying the cost of the sales and the expenses. If the business can reduce its expenses, relative to turnover, the net profit margin will improve.

Current ratio is a solvency ratio that compares current assets to current liabilities. It is a simple way of measuring how easy it would be to pay liabilities. A current ratio of 1.3:1 would mean for every £1 owed the business can quickly convert £1.30 into cash.

The **acid test ratio** is used to measure solvency in a business where stock is not always easy to convert into cash.

Asset turnover measures sales revenue relative to net assets. It shows how effectively the assets are being used.

The **debtors' collection period** (also known as **debtor days**) is a ratio that measures the average time debtors take to pay their outstanding balances. It is better that the debtor days get shorter than longer.

Creditor's payment days (also known as **creditor days**) measures the average number of days it takes a business to pay its creditors. The longer this is then the better for the cash flow of the business; however, a business may upset its suppliers if it delays payments too long and gets a bad reputation.

If your **stock turnover** gets lower then it is taking you longer to shift your stock. You may have too much stock. You should compare your stock turnover with the average for similar businesses.

The **earnings per share** measures how much profit each share earns. You would look at this to compare rates of return from alternative investments. You would want this figure to be high.

The **price earnings ratio** measures the current market price divided by the earnings per share. This shows the number of years' earnings an investor is prepared to pay in order to buy a share. The higher the figure the more confidence investors have in the business and the expectations of future profits.

Testing times: AQA

The following questions are adapted from AQA tests.

	Assessment evidence
E2	Identify different stakeholders and explain their interests in gaining financial information about the business
E5	Identify elements of working capital, cash flow and budgeting
C2	Explain why different groups of stakeholders may interpret data about the financial performance of a business in different ways
C7	Explain how businesses manage their working capital
A5	Justify changes to business practices to achieve required cash flow and budget requirements

> Susan Mann intends to open a catering business in her home town of Poole. Her idea is to supply sandwiches, rolls and cakes to employees working in businesses throughout the town. To encourage large firms to use her services she has decided to offer some customers two months' trade credit. As part of her financial planning she has drawn up a cash flow forecast for the first six months' trading.

Susan Mann's Cash Flow forecast

Income/expenditure	In £					
	January	February	March	April	May	June
Cash sales	1200	1400	1500	1850	1795	2080
Credit sales	0	0	3250	4100	4250	5500
Total cash inflow	1200	1400	4750	5950	6045	7580
Wages and salaries	450	450	600	600	600	750
Raw materials	1850	2400	3050	4150	4300	4550
Rent and rates	500	500	500	500	500	500
Total cash outflow	2800	3350	4150	5250	5400	5800
Net cash flow	−1600	−1950	600	700	645	1780
Opening balance	1000	−600	−2550	−1950	−1250	−605
Closing balance	−600	−2550	−1950	−1250	−605	1175

1 **Complete the cash flow forecast by entering the correct figures into the shaded boxes.**

2 marks

Assessment evidence: E5

| **Help!** | A straightforward question which shows that you understand the make up of cash flow. |

Answer

The opening balance for one month is always the previous month's closing balance. The net cash flow for a month is the total cash inflow minus the total cash outflow.

...and forecasting cash flow

page 78 shows you how to work it out.

2 Identify three stakeholders who may be interested in
the information shown in the cash flow forecast above.   **3 marks**

Assessment evidence: E2

 Help! Think about what cash flow tells you and who it affects.

Answer

As well as the managers within the business itself, people representing
the business's banks, suppliers and trade customers would be
interested in the cash flow forecast.

Who's interested in the accounts? page 46 shows you how to work it out.

Keeping the wolf from the door page 84 shows you how to work it out.

---

3 Explain how one of the stakeholders may want to use the
information in the cash flow forecast.   **3 marks**

Assessment evidence: C2

Help! Chose the one you know most about! Use the pages above to help.

Answer

Susan may wish to use the bank for a loan or overdraft. The bank
would need to look at her forecast to check up on what her needs
would be and to see whether she would be able to pay it back. Since
the forecast is an estimate for an untried business, the bank would
also wish to see other elements of her planning. It would want to
know, for example, whether the orders from credit sales were firm.
Creditors will want to know that the business can pay its bills. They
may cease supplies if there is uncertainty.
Customers will be especially interested if they have to put down a
deposit. If cash flow is worrying, goods may not be delivered which
will affect production processes, sales etc.

Who's interested in the accounts? page 46 explains stakeholders.

Keeping the wolf from the door page 84 gives an overview of cash flow.

---

4 Discuss the actions that Susan might take in response to the
information provided in the cash flow forecast.   **7 marks**

Assessment evidence: C7, A5

Help! Think about how Susan can either increase the inward flow of cash or slow the
outward flow. Show that you can use these ideas to evaluate Susan's position.

Answer

Susan has predicted a negative closing balance for the first five
months of trading. This must be covered. One easy way would be to
take out an additional loan for six months for around about £3000.
This would allow £500 extra if sales were slower than expected.
However, for two months she predicts her shortfall is only around
£600. Another option would be to arrange an overdraft facility with
the bank. Although the interest is higher, it is only payable on the
amount overdrawn. She could adjust her plan to reduce credit offered
to customers to one month which would put her into a cash flow
surplus in February. However, she may lose customers this way. She
should try to arrange trade credit from her suppliers which would
delay her payments for raw materials.

Keeping the cash going page 82 shows you how to work it out.

Keeping the wolf from the door page 84 shows you how to work it out.

CASH FLOW MANAGEMENT AND BUDGETING

Testing times: Edexcel

The following questions are adapted from Edexcel tests.

Assessment evidence	
E2	Identify different stakeholders and explain their interests in gaining financial information about the business
E5	Identify elements of working capital, cash flow and budgeting
C2	Explain why different groups of stakeholders may interpret data about the financial performance of a business in different ways
C7	Explain how businesses manage their working capital
A5	Justify changes to business practices to achieve required cash flow and budget requirements

Petrel Ltd is a small business which has prepared the following cash flow forecast as an estimated summary of the next 6 months' trading. Notice that all customers are receiving 2 months' credit.

	March	April	May	June	July	August
Opening bank balance	12 000	7950	−500	2050	1600	5150
Total receipts	4000	4000	12 000	9000	11 000	10 000
Total payments	8050	12 450	9450	9450	7450	7450
Closing balance	7950	−500	2050	1600	5150	7700

1 **Complete the cash flow forecast by entering figures in the shaded areas.** **2 marks**

Assessment evidence: E5

 A straightforward question which shows that you understand the make up of cash flow.

Answer

The opening balance in March is calculated by adding the total payments and the closing balance. This comes to £16 000 and must equal the receipts (£4000) plus the opening balance.

The June closing balance is calculated by adding the June opening balance of £2050 to the total receipts of £9000 and then taking away the total payments of £9450.

The July opening balance must be the same as the June closing balance.

2 **Explain fully why it is necessary for Petrel Ltd to take corrective action as a result of preparing this cash flow forecast – using an example to illustrate the effects of not taking action.** **3 marks**

Assessment evidence: C7

 This question is asking you to consider the implications of cash flow problems.

Answer

The cash flow forecast is an estimate of what the business sees as its cash needs. If this forecast turned out to be true the business would be short of cash by £500 in April although it would go on to have a significant cash surplus by August. Unless corrective action is taken, the business will be unable to pay its bills and might be forced

...and forecasting cash flow

page 78 shows you how to work it out.

into liquidation. The corrective action Petrel should take is to arrange a bank overdraft. It should also arrange to deposit the cash surplus in an interest-bearing account.

---

3 **Petrel Ltd is considering reducing the credit period given from two months to one month. Justify this change by analysing the effect it would have on the cash flow of the business. Identify key changes in the cash flow forecast which would support your answer. Include in your discussion any drawbacks associated with this policy change.** **4 marks**

Assessment evidence: E2, C2, A5

Help! Look at the credit period as a way of speeding up the working capital cycle. You are asked to consider the effect on the figures and how it might go wrong.

Answer

If Petrel reduced the credit period to one month it would receive £12 000 in April compared with the £4000 it would otherwise get. The cash flow would then be healthy in all months. There would be no need to take out an overdraft. However, reducing the credit period may alienate Petrel's customers who may decide to go elsewhere. Petrel would do well to consult its customers before taking such action.

---

4 **Complete the variance analysis summary by filling in the shaded boxes. Explain why the variance for labour was £0.** **6 marks**

Assessment evidence: E5, C7

Help! Variances show where the plans have gone wrong. By spotting them, action can be taken quickly. You have to spot them and work them out.

> Metallix is an engineering firm making a range of metal pipe systems. It operates a standard costing for all jobs. Below is the standard cost for job 102. Note: the standard cost is the estimated cost of the job.

Standard cost card for job number 102

Standard (estimated) cost		Actual cost	
Raw material thickness to be used	3mm	Raw material thickness to be used	2.5mm
Number of metres needed	25	Number of metres needed	30
Cost per metre of metal	£2.50	Cost per metre of metal	£2.40
Number of labour hours	6	Number of labour hours	4
Labour rate per hour	£5.00	Labour rate per hour	£7.50

Answer

Job 102	Standard usage	Standard cost/rate	Total standard cost	Actual usage	Actual cost/rate	Actual cost	Variance	Favourable/ adverse
Labour	6 hours	£5 per hour	£30.00	4 hours	£7.50 per hour	£30.00	£0	–
Metal	25m	£2.50	£62.50	30m	£2.40	£72	£9.50	adverse

Although the job did not take as long as budgeted for, it had to be completed by a more skilled employee whose rate is higher. The higher pay rate was exactly compensated for by the reduced time, so that the actual cost matched the estimated cost.

Keeping the cash going page 82 looks at working capital and cash flow.

Keeping the wolf from the door page 84 explains the working capital cycle.

Right or wrong? page 80 explains how to monitor the budget.

Testing times: OCR

The following questions are adapted from OCR tests.

Assessment evidence	
E2	Identify different stakeholders and explain their interests in gaining financial information about the business
E5	Identify elements of working capital, cash flow and budgeting
C2	Explain why different groups of stakeholders may interpret data about the financial performance of a business in different ways
C7	Explain how businesses manage their working capital
A5	Justify changes to business practices to achieve required cash flow and budget requirements

...and forecasting cash flow
page 78 shows you how to
work it out.

1   What is a cash flow forecast and why is it important?   **4 marks**

Assessment evidence: E5

 Help! A straightforward question which shows that you understand the make up of cash flow.

Answer

A cash flow forecast shows the movements of cash in and out of a business over a period of time. If a business starts with no cash and debts need paying before payments are made by customers, the business will be in trouble as it will be unable to pay its bills.

If the situation cannot be resolved, by borrowing money, for example, the business will become insolvent and have to cease trading.

> Sam was recently appointed as finance and administration manager at CD Productions Ltd. He produced a sales budget on to which some of the actual figures have been added.

Building a budget... page 76
explains the component
parts.

2   What sources of financial information could Sam have used to estimate the budget figures shown below?   **4 marks**

Assessment evidence: E5

 Help! Look at the component parts of a budget. Identify which are estimates and which are based on evidence.

Answer

Sam would have used historical evidence to help produce the budget below. He might have used sales figures from previous months and looked at the trends in sales. Were sales seasonal? The selling price might have been estimated from past costs plus a percentage added on for profit.

3 Use the data provided to calculate the variances between the budget and actual figures and write these in the shaded boxes.

4 marks

Assessment evidence: E5

Right or wrong? page 80 explains how to monitor the budget.

Help! The number sold was lower than forecast but the selling price was higher than expected and more than compensated for the drop in sales. Consequently, sales income was higher than budgeted for. The following two questions ask why this has happened and what its effects are.

CD Productions Ltd sales budget

	Nov-00			Dec-00		
	Budget	Actual	Variance	Budget	Actual	Variance
No. units sold	80 000	78 500	−1500	85 000	82 000	−3000
Selling price	£2.50	£2.60	£0.10	£2.50	£2.60	£0.10
Sales income	£200 000	£204 100	£4100	£212 500	£213 200	£700

4 Explain why the variances between the units sold and the selling price might have occurred.

4 marks

Assessment evidence: C7

Answer

The higher price charged might have been due to a rise in costs. Perhaps suppliers raised their prices or it took longer to produce the items so the wage budget increased. The higher price might have produced the fall in demand. The competition might have been tougher.

5 Explain how these variances might affect the calculation of budget figures for the next few months.

4 marks

Assessment evidence: C7

Help! This answer follows on from the answer to question 4.

Answer

Sam would need to find out exactly why the costs rose. If these cost rises were beyond the business's control, Sam would be able to adjust future budget figures to take these into account. Sam would look at the trends of sales and make adjustments according to the trends. He would also meet with others to see if there was anything the business could do to increase the sales.

Name three groups of stakeholders who would be interested
in Sam's cash flow forecast shown below. **3 marks**

Who's interested in the accounts? page 46 identifies the stakeholders.

Assessment evidence: E2

 Help! A straightforward question testing your general knowledge of stakeholders.

Answer

CD Productions' bank would definitely need to see the cash flow, as well as trade customers and suppliers to the business.

Cash flow forecast	November	December	January
Income			
Sales	200 000	212 500	220 000
Other	0	0	0
Total	**200 000**	**212 500**	**220 000**
Expenditure			
Rent	10 000	10 000	10 500
Utilities	1000	10 000	2000
Purchases	150 000	140 000	145 000
Wages/salaries	25 000	27 000	26 000
Motor expenses	5000	15 000	15 000
Insurance	1000	3000	3000
Other (including marketing)	500	50 000	500
Total	**192 500**	**255 000**	**202 000**
Opening bank balance	5500	13 000	−29 500
Surplus/deficit of income – expenditure	7500	−42 500	18 000
Closing balance	13 000	−29 500	−11 500

Wages for December includes Xmas bonus.

Other in December includes purchase of new machinery.

---

7 For two of these stakeholders, explain their interest and how they might react to the negative cash flows in December and January. **6 marks**

Keeping the wolf from the door page 84 shows an overview of cash flow.

Assessment evidence: C2, C7, A5

Help! Draw a quick flow diagram showing the links from stakeholder to business.

Answer

The bank will want to know if the business can pay back any loans when due.

The suppliers will want to know if the business will be able to settle the bills on time and just how much at risk the business is from going into liquidation. The suppliers will want to be sure of getting the money due to them before accepting an order.

Both stakeholders would want to know if it is sensible to pay the Xmas bonus. This, however, is not the main cause of the cash flow crisis. That is down to the purchase of new machinery. The bank would suggest either taking out a loan or arranging an overdraft for up to £30 000. The business should be able to clear the overdraft in three months. The supplier would insist that a suitable financial arrangement was made with the bank before doing business with CD Productions Ltd.

Testing times: practice questions

1 Calculate the variances set out in the table below.

Standard cost card for job number 22			
Standard (estimated) cost		Actual cost	
Quantity needed in units	100	Quantity needed in units	120
Cost per metre of metal	£2	Cost per metre of metal	£2
Number of labour hours	21	Number of labour hours	18
Labour rate per hour	£9	Labour rate per hour	£10

Job 22	Standard usage	Standard cost/rate	Total standard cost		Actual usage	Actual cost/rate	Actual cost	Variance	Favourable/ adverse
Labour	hours	£9 per hour	£			£　　per hour	hours	£	£
Metal	units	£	£						

2 Which variance to the budget would be regarded as adverse and which as favourable?

3 What is the overall variance for this job?

4 Beside the manager, what stakeholders would be interested in seeing these variances and why?

Product destination	Actual value of sales in 1999 in £	Actual value of sales in 2000 in £	Sales target 2001 in £	Actual sales 2001 in £	Variance in £	Favourable or adverse
UK	2 000 000	1 900 000	1 800 000	1 700 000		
Exports to Europe	500 000	550 000	600 000	700 000		
Exports to USA	200 000	200 000	200 000	250 000		

5 Calculate the variances for each sales area and identify whether these were favourable or adverse.

6 Which market areas are growing and which are declining?

7 Evaluate how the business may use this information to improve its performance.

8 How would a bank view these figures if the business wanted to obtain a loan for expansion?

Murrays Ltd is a small business about to start trading in March. Murrays Ltd has prepared the following cash flow forecast for its first 6 months' trading. It estimates that cash sales will be around £5000 a month. All other sales are credit sales.

	March	April	May	June	July	August
Opening bank balance	9000	4000	–2000	–1000	2500	
Total receipts		5000	13 000	15 000	14 000	15 000
Total payments	10 000	11 000	12 000	11 500		12 300
Closing balance	4000		–1000	2500	4500	

9 Complete the cash flow forecast by entering figures in the shaded areas.

10 What is the trade credit period?

11 In which month or months is there likely to be a cash flow problem?

12 Explain two possible causes of the cash flow problem.

13 What options are open to Murrays to correct the negative cash flow?

14 What would you recommend Murrays do to solve this cash flow problem?

Index